Seven Secrets
of Inspired Leaders

Seven Secrets
of Inspired Leaders

How to achieve extraordinary results
by the leaders who are doing it

Phil Dourado & Phil Blackburn

An Inspired Leaders Network book

Published in 2005 by Capstone Publishing Limited (a Wiley Company), The Atrium, Southern Gate Chichester, West Sussex, PO19 8SQ, England
Phone (+44) 1243 779777

Email (for orders and customer service enquires): cs-books@wiley.co.uk
Visit our Home Page on www.wiley.co.uk or www.wiley.com

Other Wiley Editorial Offices

John Wiley & Sons, Inc. 111 River Street, Hoboken, NJ 07030, USA
Jossey-Bass, 989 Market Street, San Francisco, CA 94103-1741, USA
Wiley-VCH Verlag GmbH, Pappellaee 3, D-69469 Weinheim, Germany
John Wiley & Sons Australia, Ltd, 33 Park Road, Milton, Queensland, 4064, Australia
John Wiley & Sons (Asia) Pte Ltd, 2 Clementi Loop #02-01, Jin Xing Distripark, Singapore 129809
John Wiley & Sons Canada Ltd, 22 Worcester Road, Etobicoke, Ontario, Canada, M9W 1L1

Wiley also publishes its books in a variety of electronic formats. Some content that appears in print may not be available in electronic books.

Library of Congress Cataloging-in-Publication Data is available

British Library Cataloguing in Publication Data

A catalogue record for this book is available from the British Library

ISBN 1841126500

Typeset in Meridien by Sparks (www.sparks.co.uk)
Printed and bound in Great Britain by TJ International Ltd, Padstow, Cornwall
This book is printed on acid-free paper responsibly manufactured from sustainable forestry in which at least two trees are planted for each one used for paper production.
10 9 8 7 6 5 4 3 2 1

Contents

The seven secrets (plus one)

Secret 1

Leadership is viral: pass it on

People want to lead their own lives. Inspired leaders give others the context, the resources and the support they need, and they let them get on with it. Your job, paradoxically, is to create more leaders, not followers. Inspired leadership is viral leadership.

Secret 2

You're not fooling anyone

You are naked: get used to it. This is the era of leadership in a gold-fish bowl. Information transparency and the erosion of deference means that if you who want to move up to the level of inspired leaders, you have to ditch the games, and find the authentic, naked you. Dare to be bare. You actually have no choice. The Emperor has no clothes.

Secret 3

They have to want to follow you

Ah, the joy of work. What's that you say? Not at your place? Then you need to re-invent work; or, at least, expand the meaning of work. To engage your people's energies and talents, inspired leaders make people an offer they can't refuse. You're a creator of meaning, a re-recruiter.

Secret 4

Make a difference

Literally. Leaders used to lead the making of things or services. Inspired leaders lead the making of difference. We have gone beyond competition to *surpetition*, as lateral thinker Edward De Bono calls it. When everything in the marketplace looks increasingly the same, *different* stands out like colour in a sea of grey. How to lead innovation: here's where you start.

Secret 5
Lead from the edge

Inspired organizations are edgy. The action takes place on the frontline, where the customers are, not in the middle, where the senior management team huddle together for warmth … and to keep an eye on each other. Inspired leaders take themselves to the edge.

Secret 6
There's nothing out there

Still see global business in terms of geographic boundaries, import/ export, a home territory and the regions? That's s-o-o-o last century. Inspired leaders see the world differently. It's not out there. It's all around you. Local is global. There's a new global soup and you're standing in it; it's lapping at the edges of your desk. Come on in; the water's lovely.

Secret 7
The impossible isn't

'Impossible' just means something that hasn't been done yet. Or even imagined. Hannibal. Elephants. Mountains. Who'd have thought it possible? Well, he did. And then made it so. Turn to this chapter for inspiration on how to think the unthinkable and lead the undoable.

Conclusion and Bonus Secret 8
Get an NBA, not an MBA

Inspired leaders architect their organizations differently: They're upside down, in many cases; inside out in others. You need a New Business Architecture. And that includes a new social architecture, too.

Why inspired leadership?

Being inspired is a virus. It raises the temperature of an organization. Inspired leaders vibrate. And their organizations resonate with them. It's almost palpable.

We all know one or two organizations that hum with purpose and conviction. When you come into their field of attraction, you instantly feel the higher energy levels, the focus, sense of commitment and confidence. You see it in people's faces and their body language; hear it in their voices. There's a buzz generated by inspired organizations that refuses to be contained: inspiration spreads up and down their supply chains; thrums down their telephone wires and crackles across their Internet connections. It's wildfire, it's lightning in a bottle.

But, there aren't that many inspired organizations around, are there? When you look at what people are capable of and then at the mediocrity most organizations bring out in them, clearly something isn't quite right. Why is that?

We're convinced it's bad leadership. The 1990s were about management. The 2000s are about leadership. But most of the leadership around at the moment is insipid, self-serving, ego-driven stuff. It's more David Brent from BBC TV's *The Office* than it is Nelson Mandela. We can't get away with this anymore.

We live in inflationary times. Last century an organization could get by, just by being good. Now, as Jim Collins has taught us,[1] you have to be *great* to stand out in a crowded, over-supplied world. Since 1989, millions of managers have been aiming for *highly-effective*, with the help of Dr Covey's *The Seven Habits* … Fifteen years on, he came up with an eighth habit and, once again, it's about moving up to great.[2] Begin to notice a pattern here? Good enough no longer is.

Leadership as usual won't deliver the extraordinary results you need to compete at this higher level. Because leadership as *usual* confines and limits people. Time for some leadership as *unusual*. Time for some *inspired* leadership.

Phil Dourado & Phil Blackburn

Acknowledgements

Thank you to INSEAD's Hazel Hamelin and bright.co.uk's Marion Janner for their helpful comments on early drafts of this book, and to Ailsa Kaye for last minute inspiration.

A book of many authors

This book has many authors. You need a critical mass to achieve any kind of change. So we looked for some of the most inspired leaders out there, and brought them together into a network; a mix of 800 or so business and not-for-profit leaders, each with a glint in their eye and a higher body temperature than most. You should feel the room hum when we bring them together (or the ether hum when they trade inspired leader practices online).

The creation of the Inspired Leaders Network was itself inspired by the work of Tom Peters. The Network's members and associates range from mould-breaking entrepreneurial leaders like *Pret A Manger* founder **Sinclair Beecham,** *YO! Sushi* founder **Simon Woodroffe** and *The Body Shop* founder **Anita Roddick ...**

...to radical bankers (yes, there are some) like **Mike Harris**, the founding CEO at the world's first telephone-only bank, *First Direct* (now helping to lead the online bank *Egg*); from sector-hopping leaders like the former CEO of the *Eurostar Group*, **Hamish Taylor ...**

... to public sector leaders like **Paul Strassmann**, one-time CIO of the US Department of Defense, **Mary Jo Jacobi**, senior trade adviser to not one but two US presidents, and **Geoff Mulgan,** until recently head of strategy in the UK Prime Minister's Policy Unit.

Our network of members and associates also includes pathfinders – business thought leaders – such as **Don Peppers** (of 1 to 1 fame), **Warren Bennis (**the 'Dean of Leadership' according to *Forbes Magazine***), Seth Godin** (*Permission Marketing*) and the digital guru **Don Tapscott.**

We do have some women leaders contributing their techniques to this book. But, not as many as we'd like: **Dianne Thompson,** CEO of the world's largest lottery operator, *Camelot*; **Larissa Joy,** European COO of *Weber Shandwick*, recently named a 'global leader of tomorrow' by the World Economic Foundation in its annual *leaderfest* at Davos; **Wendy Thomson**, who heads up the public sector reform unit in the UK government's Cabinet Office, as well as the notable names mentioned above, are among the women leaders who have contributed to the Network's pool of inspired thinking and practice.

What unites the members and friends of our Network is a commitment to achieving extraordinary results by practising leadership as unusual. Their community of interest is based on a common understanding that command and control-type leadership no longer works. They use our Network to share what they've discovered as they experiment with non-traditional forms of leadership designed to inspire extraordinary results.

We call this process 'learning from the future'. That's not as pretentious as it sounds. As the cyberpunk novelist William Gibson told us, the future is already here. It's just not evenly distributed yet. The authors of this book have distilled some of the most potent, inspired leadership juice that flowed from our Network of 800-odd leaders (some of whom are indeed odd – in a good way), dipped their pens in it, and used it to write this book.

You will find dotted throughout the book personal checklists, tips, proven (if sometimes off-the-wall) practices and advice from a number of our pioneering 'been there, done that' members and friends. Feel free to use and adapt them. As **Picasso** (an honorary, but clearly posthumous member) said:

> **'Good artists copy. Great artists steal.'**

If you want to join our Network, you can find out more about us at www.inspiredleaders.com. It's a two-way street of course: we're an inspired leadership exchange, a marketplace where you will be expected to trade insights, experiences, tips and techniques. Who knows: they may end up in our next book.

Meenu Bachan, CEO, Inspired Leaders Network

Leadership is viral: pass it on

This chapter in 30 seconds

Leadership is the new management. Last century was about the rise of organizational management. The opening years of this century are about leadership.

The single most important factor that most employees would like to see in their leader is inspiration. The problem is, there isn't nearly enough of it about. And growth is stalling as a direct result.

Only one in ten people report that their leader is inspirational. Inspired leadership is as rare and powerful as bottled lightning.

You don't have to be loud and proud to be inspirational. Quiet leaders can inspire, too. It's not an either/or question.

Leaders don't create followers. They create more leaders. Inspired is inspiring. Leadership is viral.

Example isn't just important in a leader. Example is all. Example is the carrier for the inspiration virus. Pass it on …

Leadership is viral: pass it on

Where have all the leaders gone?

'Absent Without Leave is the answer, according to a study which shows that most of us despair of meeting a manager who also qualifies as a leader.

The study ... argues that a lack of inspiration stifles businesses. It says workers and line managers are calling out for corporate leaders who inspire their staff ...

The report, 'Inspired Leadership, an Insight Into People Who Inspire Exceptional Performance',[1] identifies the three main characteristics that employees long to see:

- Genuine shared vision from executives (79% of the workers polled).
- Leaders showing confi dence and trust in their teams (77%).
- Respect from line managers and customers (73%).

The single most important factor that a majority of employees would like to see in their leader is "inspiration". However, only one in ten respondents felt that they witnessed this elusive quality at work.'

The Guardian *newspaper October, 2004*

Only one in ten! Inspired leadership seems to be rarer than hen's teeth, as exotic as bottled lightning.

It's the same around the world: the Gallup Organization's global research on employee engagement finds that 29% of employees are engaged, 55% are not engaged, and 16% are actively disengaged. This data is based on more than three million employees. Gallup estimates that just the 16% actively disengaged in the United States cost $350 billion per annum in lost productivity.[2]

This perception of a widespread absence of inspirational leadership isn't just bottom-up. It's top-down, too; in IBM's 2004 global survey of CEOs, designed to find out what was keeping the top guys awake at night, 60% of CEOs of large organizations reported their employees lacked the right expertise or leadership qualities to manage growth. 'They told us they had been focusing so hard over recent years on efficiencies and cutting costs that they had neglected the development of a next generation of leaders that would take the organization forward; at the top of their agenda now is the need for people who can inspire growth', Abigail Tierney, one of the survey report's authors, told us.

The best of times, the worst of times

For leaders in business in particular, this is the best of times and the worst of times. 'In terms of power and influence, you can forget the church, forget politics. There is no more powerful institution in society now than business', says Dame Anita Roddick, founder of The Body Shop, herself a pioneering business leader. Yet, the reputation of business and business leadership in the opening years of this century is about as low as it can go.

The comedian Steven Wright says he has a friend who is a limbo master; he can limbo so low he limbos under rugs. In the popular mind, particularly of those millions of citizen-investors who felt themselves so betrayed by the market collapse at the end of the last century, and of company employees  who find their pension contributions have disappeared into a black hole, that's about where you'd find business leadership's reputation – with the dust and furballs – so low, its disappeared under the rug.

How business leaders are portrayed in popular culture gives us some clues as to where they rank in the public mind. It's hardly inspiring. Despite all the Jack Welch-inspired talk of 'Bossless leadership', the corporate leader in popular culture is, inevitably, 'the Boss'…

> **'There is a collective consciousness about what bosses are and do and not a lot of it works in your favour. Who's the boss in the most popular television programme in the western world? Mr Burns in the Simpsons: a cheat, a changeling.'**
> *David Firth, author of* The Corporate Fool *and co-author,* Corporate Voodoo

So, there's the overtly dangerous Mr Burns. Then there's the low-level but destructive cynicism of David Brent – the dysfunctional boss in BBC TV's *The Office* – who spouts leadership platitudes while stepping all over his people and failing his way to the top, before ultimately being seen for what he is and thrown out. Ricky Gervais' grotesque fictional manager and would-be leader touched a nerve on both sides of the Atlantic.

The leader as bad guy

The movie *The Corporation* and its accompanying book, *The Corporation: The Pathological Pursuit of Profit and Power,* clung onto the coat-tails of the post-Enron mood and projected a generalized picture of psychopathic tendencies in large organizations and those who run them. From Donald Trump's portrayal of leader-as-sorcerer in the TV 'documentary' series *The Apprentice* to the emergence of the global business leader as the villain in the Bond movies after the fall of the Soviet Union, the examples of not just uninspired but downright malevolent leaders are endless.

This casting of business leader as bad guy is part of a broader loss of faith in leaders of all kinds as people look to themselves to protect their own interests, rather than expecting their elected representatives or employers to do so. One of our members calls this phenomenon 'the growth of the self-preservation society'.[3] If corporations were people (and, legally, they *are* people, interestingly: a corporation as a legal entity has the attributes and responsibilities of a person), then the dominant portrayal of big business and its leaders in our popular culture is as people whose behaviour often leads others to be wary of trusting them.

It doesn't help when psychologists come up with widely-publicized profiles that draw parallels between the character traits of psychopaths and political or business leaders.

> 'If you're bright ... you have been brought up with good social skills and you don't want to end up in prison, you probably won't turn to a life of violence. Rather, you'll ... use your psychopathic tendencies more legitimately by getting into positions of power and control. What better place than a corporation?'

says Robert Hare, a psychology professor at the University of British Columbia, who claims psychopaths can be found throughout the upper echelons of management and leadership.[4] Corporate psychopaths, says Hare, tend to be:

> 'Impulsive, arrogant, manipulative, callous, impatient, unreliable, and prone to fly into rages. They break promises, take credit for the work of others and blame everyone else when things go wrong. Wherever you get power, prestige and money, you will find them. They are smooth, polished, engaging and often charismatic.'

Hare's research suggests faster-moving, change-oriented companies are more exciting places, therefore more attractive to psychopaths.

The leader as psychopath is a sideshow, a marginal problem within the overall failure of leaders to inspire. But, the widespread coverage of such findings suggest they strike a chord; that dysfunctional David Brent-style leadership is closer to the norm most people experience in the workplace than inspired leadership, experienced by just 11%. Those who reported that their leaders were not inspired were asked to come up with words that described them. The two most common were 'ambitious' and 'knowledgeable'.[5] Today's leaders seem more focused on their own careers than those of their direct reports.

How did we get to this?

Let's look backwards a little before we go forwards. Since it was founded in 1999, the Inspired Leaders Network has focused on identifying leaders who are blueprinting how business will be done as this century unfolds, just as Henry Ford, Frederick Winslow Taylor and their peers defined 20th century business.

Economic historians have studied so-called 'long waves' of economic growth – Kondratieff cycles and the like. In these 50–60 year waves – the Victorian machine age, the post-World War II boom – powerful new management techniques are diffused across the economy, often pioneered in one sector and then adapted to others, contributing to a huge accumulation of capital.

Historically, as each wave of capital accumulation comes to an end, you tend to find the sparks of new technologies, new organizational forms and new ways of leading those new organizational forms, nestling in the embers. Some of them fail to ignite. Others consume themselves in their own fire – obvious examples from recent history would be the money-burning dotcoms and Enron's clever financial engineering seeping into fraud.

The rise of management

But, the most robust of the leading-edge changes succeed. As with natural evolution, these successful changes in the organization of production and distribution tend to become dominant. They replicate across sectors to become the genetic blueprint, the accepted form of business, for a given Age. That is how the last half of the 20th century saw the rise of modern management science from the seeds of Fordism and Taylorism. At worst, the spread of productionist thinking leads to people gaming the system – cheating to survive – as principles from a factory age are applied inappropriately to call centres, banks, hospitals and other workplaces where the unit of production being measured bears little relation to the value being delivered.

'The revolution that happened in factories and offices over a century ago has changed the way we all work', says Anita Roddick, founder of The Body Shop and a friend of our network. 'Managers have been measuring obsessively ever since, and everything, from call centres to school performance tables, owes something to Taylor.'[6]

As the 20th century closed, improved management was increasingly seen as insufficient to provide a leap forward in performance. Good management is fine in stable times, because it is all about predictability and repeatability. After decades of enhancing productivity, rightsizing, customer focus programmes, ISO9000, benchmarking, Six Sigma, Business Process Re-engineering and all that good (and not so good) stuff, every organization had come to look, well, samey. And the pace of change in markets had accelerated.

Pareto's 80/20 rule had started to bite. There is little advantage left to be squeezed out when everyone is following the same operational improvement paths, and has been for decades. Managerial capitalism appears to have outlived the society it was once designed to serve, argue James Maxmin and Shoshana Zuboff in their book *The Support Economy*. And it's a pretty powerful argument. Not least because today's individuals want and expect more than to be performance-managed.

You're not the Boss of me

Just as management is running out of steam as an improvement path, switching horses (and metaphors) to traditional leadership as an alternative growth mechanism has become a non-option, too. Traditional notions of leadership and followership presuppose a readiness to give up control to an external authority figure. And, increasingly, people won't.

The economic trends outlined above have coupled with the emergence of more educated and assertive workers and consumers; better informed, and with a strong sense of their own needs and rights. The result: a loss of deference to corporations and institutions and to people who claim authority or a position of leadership.

Yes, you can still rule some people by diktat and fear. But, that's ruling, not leading. And, since the greatest force in the universe is the need to be in control of our own lives (or denial, depending on whom you listen to), command-and-control leadership will get people to show up in body but not, crucially, in spirit. At best you'll get compliance, when what you need to drive an organization is commitment. And you won't get fulfilled people. As Publius said, 'The height of misery is to depend on another man's will'.

> **'The authoritarian leader feels their job is partly about keeping people in their place. The inspired leader feels their job is at least partly to put them in yours'.**
>
> *Meenu Bachan, CEO, Inspired Leaders Network*

They have the power

The 21st century leader's paradox is this: the very act of leading is traditionally associated with stepping out in front of others and saying, 'I'll decide what we are going to do and where we are going.'

Yet, people increasingly won't be told; they want to be in control for themselves, or at least *of* themselves. People want to lead their own lives. 'Nobody gives you power. You just take it', said the comedienne Roseanne. The genie's out of the bottle. Containment won't work. Like the UN operating in a newly-created country, part of your role is to legitimize the transfer of power that, on the ground, has already happened.

Herman Melville, at the beginning of the last century, anticipated what would happen when the workers decline to be told what to do. In his short story, *Bartleby The Scrivener*, Bartleby, a previously model employee, suddenly turns *refusenik*. He answers every request from his boss with an enigmatic 'I would prefer not to'. Increasingly, 21st century employees decide if they want to. And the answer from the majority of them, according to the figures on disengagement mentioned above, is that they don't. They are simply not inspired to. (N.B. Don't make the mistake of interpreting 'inspiration' as a form of super-persuasion; of inspiration as being an unharnessed tool for old-style leadership that bends people to a leader's will).

Slackers?

One factor in the inability of leaders to engage people today is that experience no longer lends automatic authority. Anyone whose workforce includes a large proportion of Generation X-ers and Y-ers knows this more than most. Twenty-somethings tend to think they know more than their elders about the way the world works for a simple reason: it's true. When it comes to the connected, digital world, they grew up bathed in bits. And, like policemen, the

21st century cognoscenti – the clued-up generation – are getting younger all the time.

There is a demographic revolution intersecting the technology-enabled business revolution, but it is widely ignored. The baby boomers' children are the first generation to grow up digital, and 85% of them know more about the Internet and computing than their parents.[7] This is the first time that kids are the authority on something that is changing business. It's not a generation gap. It's a generation lap.

© 2002 Ted Goff

"Here, do all this work and I'll reward you by nitpicking every error you make."

They are lapping us. Too many of this generation are dismissed as slackers when they are simply disengaged. Douglas Copeland, in his novel *Generation X*, has a lot to answer for here. It was he who coined the word 'McJob'. The antidote to the Generation X-type refusal to engage must be to offer the opposite of a McJob.

Generation X and Y are, in fact, smarter, faster, more flexible in their thinking, more motivated, fresh, less jaded, more in synch with the digital age, more action-oriented and innovative than their older bosses. Who sets up the VCR and DVD player in your house? Who networks the home PCs? Who knows what's cool first?

Reverse mentoring

Where the generation that grew up in the 1960s and 1970s came home from school and switched on the TV (a passive medium), their kids have grown up interacting. It changes the way they think. They are tuned into this stuff and can use it faster and more effectively. How do you deal with this? In Finland, they hired students to teach the teachers. What about when they work for you? You will have to think of them as investors of intellectual capital rather than a cost.

Procter & Gamble introduced a reverse mentoring system where you couldn't make it into the Top 200 in the company without a mentor, who had to be under the age of 21. General Electric introduced something similar under Jack Welch. So, there are changes we need to make in the people we hold up as role models. 'We need to move away, to an extent, from these Rushmorean images of great leaders as older heroic figures', our honorary member Warren Bennis told us recently.

One of the most interesting things about IT-led companies is the way young people moved into positions of responsibility and leadership. Bill Gates was 22 when he co-founded Microsoft. Jeff Bezos was 29 (an old man in dotcom years) when he founded Amazon.

Manager or Leader

We said at the front of this book that management was last century's discipline, and leadership is this century's. But, by that we don't mean you give up on management and focus everything on leadership. Nor do we mean to suggest management is, ahem, for those who lack the imagination to be leaders; that leadership is somehow a higher evolutionary form. We just mean all the management literature and discipline is already pretty well defined and codified. It's been so well MBA'd we all know how to manage. Or, at least, how we should be managing.

> 'The purpose of a (managerial) bureaucracy is to perpetuate itself. Inspired leadership is about change. You can see how they wouldn't get on together ...'
>
> Network member Shanti Duggal, Head of eBusiness, Friends Provident

The key distinction is the obvious one that you manage things, but you lead people. That's true enough. But we're not saying the two are mutually exclusive. All the cant you hear from 'leaders' about how they're the visionaries and their job is to deal with the big picture and that 'I don't do detail', just means they're using the tag 'leadership' to dump – sorry, delegate – the hard stuff on their subordinates, while they themselves swan around proclaiming the vision. This kind of leader quickly loses touch with the reality of the business. Inspired leaders do vision. But, they also do detail. Our honorary member Warren Bennis, the Dean of Leadership (as *Forbes Magazine* calls him), puts it this way:

'As the Zen master says, first Enlightenment, then the laundry. Leadership is about both. It's not just about vision and guidance from on high. It's about delivering results'.

Warren Bennis

Leaders surf

And, yes, managers promote stability while leaders catalyze change. But you have to do both, don't you, sometimes flipping from one to the other several times in the same day. The chaotic nature of modern business – chaotic as in constantly having to change to anticipate or react to fast-changing markets, not chaotic as in undisciplined – means managers have to develop their leadership skills to help their people surf change as it comes at them. This applies to non-profit organizations, too, where the drive to change faster to keep up with changes in society provides a similar sense of struggling to keep ahead.

So, we don't subscribe to the old theory that managers are from Mars and leaders from Venus. The source of this thinking was a 1977 article by a Harvard professor, Abraham Zaleznik, who proposed this: 'Because leaders and managers are basically different, the conditions favourable to one may be inimical to the growth of the other'.[8] Well, things have evolved since 1977. We're now in the age of leadership at all levels. You can't have a flattened hierarchy without lots of mini-leaders running around inside it. And, when they're not leading, they're managing.

So what about that 'Leaders do the right things, managers do things right' quip that trips so glibly off the tongue of modern business gurus? Well, kind of. But, sound-bite polarizations are like the 'help' buttons on computers: invariably less helpful than they seem. Beware any aphorism that neatly splits things in two. The world's far messier than that. One of our members is fond of saying: 'A manager's CV will detail the things they have done. A leader's CV will detail the possibilities they create.' There is a general truth in the idea that when you are managing, you are focusing on getting things done predictably, whereas when you are leading, you are about helping others get things done, often unpredictably.

Make yourself dispensable

This focus on others rather than on the self is a defining characteristic of inspired leadership. Martin Luther King captured the essence of this with the concept of the servant-leader, which corporate gurus such as Ken Blanchard and Jan Carlzon, the turnaround CEO at Scandinavian Airline Systems, subsequently championed in the business arena.

This central dimension of inspired leadership – creating possibilities for others and inspiring people to be aware of their own ability to fulfil those possibilities – obviously isn't something we're claiming as a modern discovery. We are not trumpeting a modern form of inspired leadership (liberationist) over an old-fashioned form of expired leadership (command and control). If it doesn't sound too achingly trendy what we are actually touting here is a form of post-modern leadership.[9]

Many of the elements of inspired leadership have been around for a long time, including the need to develop independence rather than dependence on the leader. Here's some proof, from the father of Taoism, writing in the 6th century BC:

> **'The wicked leader is he who the people despise.**
> **The good leader is he who the people revere.**
> **The great leader is he of whom the people say,**
> **"We did it ourselves".'**
>
> *Lao Tsu, from the Tao Te Ching*

Or, as Sinclair Beecham, founder of Pret A Manger, told us: 'I used to think my role as a leader was to be indispensable, with the phone always ringing, showing what a good leader I was by always being there to solve problems and fight fires. Now I know my job is to stop that phone ringing. The less it rings, the more dispensable I am, the better.'

Make leaders, not followers

You make yourself dispensable by making more leaders. The role of the leader today, says the consumer rights campaigner and occasional US presidential candidate Ralph Nader, is not to create followers, but to create more leaders.

According to Apple founder Steve Jobs, Microsoft's powerful culture and epic growth was not down to Bill Gates' charisma as a leader, but his ability to create 'mini-me' leaders who drive Microsoft forward: 'Bill has done a great job of cloning himself as the company has grown. Now there are all these aggressive "Little Bills" running the various product groups and divisions, and they just keep coming at you and coming at you. They're not afraid to stumble ...'[10]

Mike Harris, executive vice-president at the European online bank Egg, says any attempt to drive transformational change from one leader at the top, or even a small group of leaders, is doomed to failure. 'I recall when we reached a point where I just couldn't see us moving forward with the speed we needed. The whole organization was running on my ability to generate transformational change. The clear answer was, we needed 30 or so leaders generating transformational change, not just me. Creating a cadre of leaders around you who can take the odd failure and not be cowed gives you an exponential growth in your organization's ability to transform itself.'

The key to spreading the leadership virus is not being afraid to help other people to achieve greater levels of control; not feeling threatened by their increased power or independence. Dianne Thompson, CEO of the world's largest lottery operator, Camelot, says you have to be enthusiastic about appointing people who are better than you are.

Developing leaders is time consuming. As Warren Bennis puts it: 'You can't put a person in a microwave and out pops the McLeader. It doesn't happen like that. Leadership evolves.' That's why Jack Welch, legendary former CEO of General Electric, spent a large proportion of his time developing GE's leaders. And it's why his successor, Jeffrey Immelt, continues to do so. How much time do you spend on it?

Reward viral leaders

Tony Highland, a leader at Barclays Bank, began rewarding his people based on their development of the people around them.

Barclays' central development unit is looking at the possibility of replicating this model across Barclays. Tony, incidentally, is an example of an action-oriented inspired leader who has the ability to create a vibrant culture within a business unit that is part of a giant, fairly slow-moving group. His secret is that he just does it. Talk to his direct reports and they tell you, reverentially, that they've never worked for anyone like him. 'It is just so liberating', said one.

Concerned that his large organization needed to channel its energies, Tony took to the road, asking all 2,167 people who reported, ultimately, to him, what kind of organization they wanted to work in. They all, more or less, wanted the same six things: challenge, responsibility, trust, reward, learning, and to have fun while doing it. They were then challenged to commit to behaving in those ways.

Leaders learn

John Stewart, CEO of National Australia Bank Group, told us this: 'When I was CEO at the Woolwich (a mid-sized UK financial services company) I noticed, as we all do, that there are branch managers who can be put into a poorly-performing branch and turn it around to top all the league tables.

So, we got ten of these leaders together for two days to find out how they do it. Let's see what they have in common, bottle it and spread it around the organization, I thought. Two days later, we realized it wasn't possible. You can't clone leadership. They all had their own leadership styles and approaches.

But, there was one thing they all had in common: they were learning from each other all the time. I watched them, and noticed that they were all writing pages and pages of notes after talking to each other. They were constantly saying 'That's a great idea!' They were enthused. They were pushing forward and getting 1% better at everything all the time.

They just kept learning from each other what works and what doesn't. Learning from the experiences of other leaders is what this generation of leaders has to do. It's how you minimize mistakes – learning what to avoid as well as what works. What you don't do is as important as what you do'.

The authors both attended a major conference where the keynote speaker was Feargal Quinn, whose chain of retail supermarkets in Ireland pioneered innovations that supermarket chains around the world – from Wal-Mart to Tesco – copied. Quinn wowed the audience at the conference with his morning keynote session. Later in the afternoon, after most keynote speakers would have disappeared, there was a small figure sitting at the back of a break-out session, scribbling furiously in a notebook. It was Feargal Quinn, multi-millionaire transformational business leader and Irish senator, still learning.

Does inspired have to mean loud?

There's a debate going on at the moment about what kind of person becomes an inspired leader. The stereotype of the inspirational leader is of someone expansive and charismatic, often highly assertive, who inspires through sheer force of personality and personal energy.

Though some inspirational leaders do fit this mould, a large number do not. Many are quiet, almost introverted. Jim Collins, in his book *Good to Great*, champions the selfless, dedicated leader as the source of long-term organizational inspiration and of the market-beating results that flow from this. Ego-free, sometimes introverted leadership is the route to sustained out-performance of the competition; that's Collins' conclusion. The implication is that charismatic has to be short-term (we're all mortal); also that the cult of personality that charisma implies can be suspect as a driving force. Charisma is close to charlatan in the dictionary.

Collins' championing of the quiet leader is loudly derided by the business guru Tom Peters (who used to be Collins' senior at McKinsey, incidentally). Peters likes his leaders loud and proud and sees a noisy force of personality (as opposed to Collins' quiet forcefulness) as a powerful aid to inspiration. As an aside, Peters is also sharp enough to say this of his own and Collins' writing: 'Whatever we say we are writing about, I am increasingly of the conviction that when we write, we write about ourselves'. Anyone who has heard

Peters speak knows which type of leader he identifies with personally, and he (Peters) says Collins' personality matches the quiet virtues of the leaders he extols in *Good to Great*.

Our own finding is that inspired leaders are drawn from both personality extremes and from all points in the middle. You can be quietly charismatic, inspired without being loud, entrepreneurial without being colourful. The one thing to watch out for with noisy charisma is falseness. As Peters himself, who champions 'being true' over corporate BS, says: 'Charismatic leadership almost always has a tyrannical side to it'.[11]

The qualities of an inspired leader

The following are some of the most commonly observed characteristics of inspiring leaders:[12]

Strong strategic focus
They are very good at ensuring that the business only does those things where it has the resources to do a good job and where it can add real value.

Lateral thinkers
They are particularly adept at drawing on experiences outside their own sectors and taking a much broader view than the norm. They look at things laterally and encourage their people to do the same.

Vision and communication
An inspirational leader has a very strong, customer-focused vision of where the business should be going. Importantly they are also able to communicate their vision so that their people feel they own it and know where they fit into it. The best leaders are great communicators who prefer plain speaking to jargon.

Principled
They are deeply committed, courageous, demanding of themselves and their people and confident, albeit often in a quiet and understated way. What singles them out is an exceptionally strong set

of values built on honesty, openness and true respect for their people.

Reflective

What distinguishes them is genuine humility and not being afraid to show vulnerability on occasions. This comes from regular periods of reflection and an unquenchable thirst for learning.

Risk takers

They have a marked tendency to 'bend the rules', take calculated risks, and, on occasions, be guided by their gut-feelings. They also tolerate this in other people, recognizing that a certain amount of flexibility is essential to adapt to circumstances and make real strides forward.

Accessible

They make time to get out and speak to people. This informal and personal contact is a very powerful motivator. Equally, when they are at their own desk, they aren't cosseted behind a wall of PAs.

Value attitude

They value skills and training very highly, but they also focus heavily on attitude, believing that without the right attitude and motivation, nothing will be achieved.

Why people respond to inspired leaders

So, if those are some of the qualities of inspired leaders, why do these traits produce results?

Pay is only one component of job satisfaction. Other factors like respect and prestige can be tremendously important in making staff feel good about their jobs. The reason that inspiring leadership produces results is that it contributes directly to fulfilling many of people's emotional needs.

The following findings[13] are some of the ways in which inspired leadership contributes to improved job satisfaction, motivation and productivity:

- **Respect:** a business where only senior managers are allowed to 'have ideas' rarely achieves great staff satisfaction. Inspirational leaders ask for, and respect, what their people tell them about how to do things better, and they provide the resources to ensure that the solutions are delivered.

> '**What creates trust, in the end, is the leader's manifest respect for the follower.'**
>
> *Jim O'Toole, in his book* Leading Change

Some inspired leaders signal their respect for employees and associates by changing the ranking of stakeholder importance. The principle of 'customer first' and 'the customer is always right', for example, may seem a sensible response to the growth in customer power. But, being ultra-flexible to accommodate the customer can have the effect of running frontline employees ragged by appearing to rank the customer's needs and rights above their own. Inspired leaders commonly make it clear that customers and employees rank together in importance – that their interests are in common. Or they explicitly establish the principle of 'employee first, customer second'. There's a great story about Gordon Bethune, CEO of Continental Airlines, that shows how powerful this principle can be when put into action by the leader in a highly-visible way:

'**Manifest respect for followers' ... an example**

On a Continental Airlines flight CEO Gordon Bethune was sitting on the flight deck chatting with the captain and first officer as the passengers were boarding. He left to take his assigned first class seat, to let the flight crew begin preparations for take-off.

A 'one pass' platinum elite member boarded the plane. Seeing several first class seats open, he began to argue with the flight attendant over why he had not been upgraded. The flight attendant said she would get a gate attendant to find out and see what could be done. The customer began swearing at her.

CEO Bethune was walking down the aisle, on his way back from the flight deck, and heard his employee being verbally abused. 'Can I help somehow?' he asked. The passenger said: 'Huh: Who the *&%@?!? are you?' Bethune replied: 'I'm the CEO of this company. May I see your ticket, sir?'

The passenger gave his ticket to Gordon, who saw a total fare of just under six hundred dollars. He pulled out his billfold, peeled off six 100 dollar bills, and placed the money in the man's hand.

Then he tore up the passenger's ticket.

'Now', Gordon said. 'You get the @?*!&?* off my airplane'.

The flight attendant could barely keep a straight face.

Source: An email circulated virally among people in the airline industry. Whether it actually happened exactly as described is not the point. Gordon Bethune had developed such a reputation as a leader who respected his people, that the email became viral because it was true to this CEO's behaviour. Even if he didn't do it, he would have done. Notably, this story was passed to one of the authors by a Virgin Atlantic employee – the story has become legend within and outside Bethune's sector, not just within Continental. It also speaks to the related issue of 'being valued' (see below).

- **Being involved** : inspirational leaders involve their people in changes. They give their people the freedom and support to get on with the job. When you walk around these companies, there is an electricity in the air – you can feel the energy and buzz. The bottled lightning is uncorked.
- **Having fun:** in successful companies, people work hard but enjoy themselves in the process. Fun is a great indicator that an organization is innovative. Fun is also a key innovation driver. At the organizations surveyed by The Great Place To Work Institute, you see a lot of fun at work.

> **'If there is one vital lesson for leaders it's this: if you're not having fun, you're not doing it right.'**
> *Sir Nicholas Montagu, until recently Chairman of the UK's Inland Revenue*

- **Being trusted** : it's no coincidence that, when you ask people what it is like to work in an organization run by an inspirational leader, they talk about openness, honesty, respect and trust (the subject matter of our next chapter). These firms can boast highly committed people who bring a great sense of responsibility to their work.

- **Being appreciated:**   recognition is an absolutely crucial element of inspiration, and few things are more powerful, or simple, than a genuine 'thank you'. Inspirational leaders know that it's vital that people feel appreciated and valued, so they show their appreciation through extensive celebration of success – both formally and informally.

- **Valuing and being valued** : the best leaders promote a culture where their people value themselves, each other, the company and the customers. Everyone understands how their work makes a difference. This helps to build a commitment to higher standards where everybody is always looking to do things better.

> **'To keep faith with staff is the only way forward.'**
> *Nigel Paine, Head of People Development, the BBC*

To end this chapter, here's an example that our network member Nigel Paine shared with us of inspired leadership in action. It pulls together many of the qualities outlined above and shows the results that can be achieved. The story revolves around the leadership of Greg Dyke, who was Director-General of the BBC for only a short period until stepping down from the job over a high-profile spat with the government about the BBC's reporting of issues leading up to the war in Iraq.

When Dyke resigned suddenly, thousands of employees massed in the street outside his office. It was spontaneous. When he came back into the offices after going out to thank them, he didn't realize that half his face was plastered with lipstick. He looked like a circus clown. 'These people just wanted to thank him for inspiring them', said Nigel Paine.

As you read it, ask yourself this question: would your people take to the streets for you in their thousands, as they did for Greg Dyke? That's not a question that speaks to your ego. It's a question about your ability to inspire and to keep faith with people. If the answer is 'no', then absorb the leadership virus from this story yourself, by noting the leader's actions that led up to the mass demonstration of inspiration at the end. And adapt and copy them.

Inspired Leadership is… when people take to the streets for you

Just imagine

After Greg Dyke became Director-General of the BBC, he announced that he had discovered two significant things about the Beeb's working culture. 'First, it's a rather unhappy place to work. Second, the people seem to be disconnected. They work in their silos and they hate each other.'

'Just imagine how great we could be if we all pulled together …' said Greg, almost as a throwaway comment. And so, the 'Just Imagine' programme was begun, in which 10,000 of the Beeb's 26,000 employees took part in a series of sessions to identify what needed to be put right. The two major findings were that management and leadership was abysmal and that most people felt disempowered and unable to reach their potential within the Beeb's stifling culture.

Reaching for dreams

We were a bit like the Empire, with 26,000 people making tea for a handful of bosses. We were inspired in what we had to do by a quote from Jack Welch, former Chairman & CEO of General Electric in the US: 'The challenge we all face is to create an environment where people can reach their dreams.'

The BBC has always been identified as one of the top five most desirable employers by graduates. Yet, it has never made it into the Sunday Times Top 100 places to work. Most people in the Beeb find they do not get close to the creative programme-making that defines it and attracted them in the first place. So, the first step to enabling people to reach their dreams was … to induct them.

No induction?

That's right: the BBC had no general induction programme. So, a compulsory one was created. Every new BBC employee now, as part of their induction, makes a TV or radio programme, or builds a website and, if they can get the tickets, will sit in the audience of a broadcast programme as it is being made.

There were people who had spent 40 years at the BBC and never got that close to the output. Five thousand people have been through it now and they love it. We take them through in waves of 90 people a week. The first group went through a year and a half ago and the networking it causes is amazing: that group still keeps in touch with each other.

This imaginative approach to induction achieved two things: it stopped people leaving shortly after joining, and it provided a sense of 'One BBC' that everyone was working for.

Values and better leadership

1,500 leaders at the BBC have been through a leadership programme, with another 4,500 following. This was as a direct result of employees saying in the Just Imagine exercise that they wanted better leaders who would help them reach their potential.

Six BBC values emerged from the constant conversations Dyke encouraged. We didn't get McKinsey in to come up with our values. They came naturally out of the internal conversations we were having. The values were:

- Trust is the foundation of the BBC. We are independent, impartial and honest
- Audiences are at the heart of everything we do
- Quality
- Creativity
- Respect
- Working together.

The values were underlined with 56 behaviours such as 'I support the best idea, not just my own or that of the person I see as most important ...'

The big brainstorm

The Big Brainstorm followed, as part of the 'Making It Happen' overall change programme. This was our first attempt at mass creativity, where 300 employees were taught creative techniques in teams that had to use those techniques to come up with a programme format. The winning format was commissioned on the spot. Then there was The Big Conversation, in which 17,000 people came together to discuss how to improve working practices – the biggest gathering in the BBC's history.

Closing the skills/innovation gap

The BBC has an impressive skills base, but that's a mile away from having an innovative culture. So, we have set about revolutionizing the BBC's intranet as our delivery vehicle for closing that gap. Staff now have access to online personal development plans, learning journeys and 360 degree feedback. learn.gateway was created as one access point for BBC people to learn and develop on the Net.

Would your people take to the streets for you?

An organization's culture is like the last truck on the train. Your engine of change may have charged around the corner, but your overall culture will be the last thing to turn that corner. It's a measure of how much momentum Greg Dyke had developed in making BBC employees feel important that, when he resigned, 8,000 of them took to the streets to show their support for him. These people just wanted to thank him for inspiring them. It was an extraordinary spontaneous outburst.

Source: Nigel Paine, Head of People Development, the BBC.

This chapter drew on the thinking and practice of the following Inspired Leaders Network members and friends:

Dame Anita Roddick
Founder, The Body Shop.

Warren Bennis
Warren is Professor and Founding Chairman of The Leadership Institute at the University of Southern California. He is also Chairman of the Center for Public Leadership at Harvard's Kennedy School. He is the author of 27 books on leadership and management. The *Financial Times* says Warren virtually invented leadership as an academic discipline.

Richard Whiteley
Co-founder, The Forum Corporation, author, *Customer-Centered Growth*, Addison-Wesley Publishing, 1996.

Tony Highland

Director of Sales & Service, Barclays Small Business & Barclays Direct. 'I'm a translator', says Tony. 'It's my job to translate what could be seen as soft, fluffy, feelgood stuff into hard business results.'

Sinclair Beecham

Co-founder, Pret A Manger. If you meet Sinclair at a party and ask him what he does for a living, he answers, 'I make sandwiches'.

Dr Abigail Tierney, Said Business School, Oxford and IBM

When Abigail did her doctorate at Oxford, she looked at how laboratories that had produced Nobel laureates reached such an exalted peak and what sort of leadership existed in them. Abigail later went on to co-author IBM's 2004 global report into the new CEO agenda, in which 60% of CEOs reported that their employees lacked the right expertise or leadership qualities to manage growth.

Euan Semple, Director of Knowledge Management Solutions, the BBC

Euan has led some extraordinary developments in the BBC's use of intranets to share inspired practices and connect people.

John Stewart, CEO of National Australia Bank Group

John, a great banking innovator, has a George Bernard Shaw quote on his desk that was a favourite of Robert Kennedy's, too. It says, 'Some men see things as they are and ask why. Others dream things that never were and ask why not.'

Don Tapscott

Don is a business strategist and entrepreneur. He is a world-leading authority on the impact of information and communication technologies. He has authored or co-authored seven books, including best-sellers such as *Digital Capital: Harnessing the Power of Business Webs*, *Growing Up Digital* and *The Digital Economy*.

Crawford Hollingworth
CEO, Headlight Vision.

Shanti Duggal
Head of eBusiness, Friends Provident.

Nigel Paine
Head of People Development, the BBC.

Dianne Thompson
CEO, Camelot, operator of the UK's National Lotto.

You're not fooling anyone

This chapter in 30 seconds

Face it; you are naked. This is the era of leadership in a goldfish bowl; leadership as reality TV, as *The Truman Show*. Your every move is watched and analyzed. You can't hide anything. Inspired leaders are comfortable naked. They've nothing to hide.

You →

You can no longer lead by virtue of having more information than anyone else, by hiding secrets or relying on deference to the authority of your job title or by projecting a fake 'you' as uber-leader. Everything is see-through.

Most people in most organizations are crying out for authenticity, for you and the organization to be True.

You have to be driven by commonly accepted values. Not for ethical reasons tacked on to your organization as an afterthought, but to build the trust and relationships that give you permission to lead.

SECRET 2

You're not fooling anyone

True story: The CEO of a major bank is having a hair-down, intimate tête-à-tête with around a hundred of his next generation leaders. These are the people he's grooming for the top. In their early 30s, mostly, they're all heads of department or business units, VPs and the like. He's got them in a small, cosy room. He's given them an hour of his time so they know how important they are to the future of this organization. He's taking questions from them; frank questions. He stands at the front of their rows of seating, but doesn't distance himself too much – he is standing with one foot placed on an empty chair in the front row, elbow on knee, leaning forward, into his audience. His body language is saying 'I'm one of you at the moment'.

He's just told them he wants them to take chances, fail sometimes; that failure is OK. They need to be leaders *and* managers (a very astute point, this), not one or the other. A glittering career should include failures. Lack of failure is a sign of fear, of no innovation.

Suddenly, 'What's your biggest failure?' asks a brave young leader from halfway back in the room. This is the defining moment of the session, though the CEO fails to pick up on it. He steps back from his intimate, confessional pose, thrusts both hands into his trouser pockets and paces back and forth in front of the answer to his long-term succession problems; the people whose trust he is about to erode without realizing it; who are about to be disappointed when they need to be inspired. He smiles as he remembers a moment.

The twist in the tale

'Ah, I remember a good one', he chuckles, puffs out his chest just a little more and proceeds to tell them a story about how he had taken his eye off the ball in the marketplace when he was about their age; had left the interest rate on a particular product fixed when wild changes in the market had led to a wave of fast responses from the competition. Everybody changed their rate but him. His colleagues were sending him panicky messages asking him what on earth he thought he was doing. Why didn't he move? He suddenly realized he had made a ghastly mistake and his bank was now exposed to heavy losses. He got ready to clear his desk and waited for the call from his boss telling him he was out.

But now, the story takes a twist. 'Suddenly, the markets turned', he says, as if telling the punch line to a joke: 'I was saved. We made a bundle. Everyone else lost out. My colleague in the office next door came in and said: "You lucky SOB! How on earth did you do that!?"'

So, what's the message this CEO has just imparted to his people? Be lucky. Don't be found out. Even when you make mistakes, end up getting it right. To get to my position, you have to be, ultimately, infallible. Talk about risk-taking and the need to get it wrong sometimes, but cover your back. If you do get it wrong, ensure the story you tell still positions you as the heroic leader who saved the day. Failure is weakness. Failure is for losers. I'm a winner. You'd better be winners, too …

> **'Strategic leadership requires a readiness to look personally foolish … and total honesty; a readiness to admit you got it wrong'.**
> *Sir John Hoskyns, founder of Hoskyns Systems*

You're on-stage

Leadership in the 21st century is like being permanently on-stage. But, you're not faced with an adoring public, throwing flowers (or underwear) at you. Your employees, investors, customers, the press, suppliers – your public – are generally wised-up and wearing x-ray specs. You can't fool them. To win their attention and respect, you have to be real. There is a deep hunger for authenticity and truth in the opening years of this century.[1] And, it's not being satisfied by organizational leaders.

That failure is played out in the small misdemeanours and disappointments that accumulate around leaders who, like our bank CEO at the top of this chapter, habitually fail to match rhetoric with behaviour.

Those incongruities, the failure to 'walk the talk', are amplified in the current climate by the damage that the reputation of business leadership has sustained, particularly in the US, with the corporate scandals of Enron, Worldcom and the like. For individual leaders, as well as companies, in a connected world, the time span from hero to zero, is remarkably fast. The size of the disparity between what you claim and what you are is directly proportional to the collapse in your share price as soon as the gap becomes public knowledge. And it will become public knowledge.

One of our members is Aidan Halligan, the England's Deputy Chief Medical Officer, who has a mischievous sense of humour. He likes telling this story:

> **'There was a huge multi-national in the US which spent millions of dollars taking all their staff away a few years ago to learn their new values. It's a *Harvard Business Review* case study, actually. They developed a new Values Statement ... designed to imbue the company's new values into their people. And the values were:**
> **Communication**
> **Respect**
> **Integrity and**
> **Excellence.**
> **You know the name of that company?**
> **Enron.'**

True cultures

Inspiration needs a true culture in which to thrive. 'True' in the sense of honest and congruous – very little slippage or disparity between words and actions. Part of Aidan's job is leading teams that turn around poorly-performing hospital units, particularly those where there may have been a high-profile crisis that the unit needs to recover from. He says that in dysfunctional workplaces it's not just leaders who practise deception – intentionally or otherwise. It seeps into the culture. To surface an organization's true culture, to bring it out of hiding, Aidan has a tool he calls a Power Map. He uses it with the board of an organization to show where the axis of power really lies.

It looks like an organization chart, but shows where the real power lines are. The chart features photos of heads of departments' faces, 'love lines' connecting those who co-operate and help each other and vendetta lines connecting departments and individuals who seem to actively work against each other. The Power Map brings the axis of real power into sharp focus – often not the official hierarchy at all, but the channels through which power flows – so the organization can move in on the axis to change it. Acknowledging the politics and manoeuvring of leaders that get in the way of the overall objective of the organization requires absolute honesty, points out Aidan.

To surface culture problems that people are blind to, Aidan's change agents equip an organization's change management team with video cameras and professional writers to capture stories and play them back. For example, one hospital consultant and his team were offended when told that they were rude to patients and junior staff as they did their rounds on the ward. Aidan's team videoed them, with the doctors' consent. When the team played the video back the consultant was stunned at the aggressive impression he and his team were giving to others.

Leadership lessons are easiest to spot in extreme examples, and this turning around of poorly performing units is just that; an extreme example of the need for an organization to be true if it has a legacy of dysfunction. The wider learning for leaders who want to replace low-level dysfunctional interference that holds back the achievement of extraordinary performance, is this: communicate the need for change using real stories. It provides the evidence to break down denial.

Spinning makes people dizzy

It is in the telling and living of true stories that the leader wins hearts and minds. The people you aspire to lead are media and soundbite

© 1999 Ted Goff

"I need to trick the staff into having good morale. Any suggestions?"

savvy. We have all grown up being marketed to. It's in our bones. We've been inoculated since childhood and know how the manipulation game works. For the sake of our own sanity, we subconsciously filter out and edit messages that could lead us down a path that is not in our interest; that our instinct doesn't immediately identify as true and well-meant. Leaders come up against those filters when competing for attention and trust.

> 'I'm totally honest with the press. When they say: "You've been talking about these Yotels (YO! branded hotels) for two years. Where are they?" I honestly say: "I haven't got my act together on that yet." The innovative brands that exist today can't be invented by an ad agency any more. You have to be real.'
>
> Simon Woodroffe, founder of Yo! Sushi, currently building an empire of Yo!

There has been an explosion in internal communications programmes that take persuasive techniques from marketing and point them at employees. We find that this approach can often be counter-productive. The problem is that if everyone, instinctively rather than rationally, knows how marketing communication works and that it is about manipulating people to change their behaviour to your advantage, then the game's up. Nobody believes the management-speak or corporate BS any more.

Devil-speak

Here's some extreme thinking to throw this into sharp relief: the comedian Bill Hicks used to have a riff in his set about marketing and advertising. He would stand on the edge of the stage and ask if there were any marketing people in the audience. 'You are the spawn of the Devil', he would tell them straight-faced. The audience would laugh. 'No, seriously. You should go away and die,' Hicks would say without the flicker of a smile.

The audience would laugh nervously again. 'Stop laughing,' Hicks would shout. 'I am seriously telling you that if you work in advertising or marketing you have no right to be on this earth with your fellow human beings, whose minds you spend all your time trying to mess up, and that you are the spawn of the Devil and you should die: Now.'

After a pause, in which the audience would grow slightly unnerved, he would add: 'And now I see one or two of you out there who look like advertising types who stopped smiling for a second. But now you are smiling again and thinking: "Ah, Bill's being clever. He's going for the anti-marketing market. Good niche to go for!" And that is why I hate you and why you are evil. Because I'm not going for any market. I simply mean it.'[2]

Increasingly, 'I simply mean it' has to be at the core of leadership and business. People will see through anything else. Being authentic enough to say what you mean is so rare (according to all those surveys on what leaders and managers do) that it will instantly win attention. And, if you've got their attention, you're halfway there.

The Attention Economy

It's not the Information Economy. Power in fact flows in a reverse direction to the flow of information. It's the Attention Economy. There's too much information, creating a noise that approaches din. It's the attention people pay to your information or message that is in short supply. That principle applies to your internal communications as much as to messages directed at customers and other stakeholders. See the work of the former theoretical physicist Michael Goldhaber for more on the power of attention. Goldhaber originally framed his argument in the context of the Net. But, it's in the context of the overloaded individual human mind that the attention economy operates.

Seth Godin and others have documented how the average American is subjected to up to 20,000 messages a day (the figure varies from around 3,000 upwards, depending on how you measure them). Gaining their attention, rather than the illusion of their attention – if you've ever been speaking to a 20-something or younger and noticed they're actually listening to their portable MP3 player while nodding in your direction, you'll know what we mean – is the foundation of building permission to lead.

Attentive leadership

You can't inspire as a leader without earning their attention. Leading smart young people, in particular, has its own challenges: 'In many cases you are dealing with people who are brilliant, but with the attention span of a gnat', says Stephen Harvey, who used to have the wonderful (and self-chosen) job title Director of People, Profit and Loyalty at Microsoft in the UK, but has reverted to Director of People and Culture. Here's Stephen's take on how to lead in a way that keeps your people's attention:

Leading attentively – how Microsoft inspires its people

Play to their strengths

Imagine a world where your people play to their strengths every day. In the average workplace only 20% of employees live in this world.[3] That's the proportion of people who said they were allowed to spend their time on what they did best. Let them do what they are best at, rather than focusing on what they don't do well. It's a guaranteed way of improving both morale and business results.

Look after your stars

It's critical to identify who your top talents are and then 'love bomb' them. I meet the top 10% of our company on a regular basis, to find out how they are doing, how they are developing and most importantly what life is like in their world. You have to let them know they are your talent and your future. But ensure it's a two-way deal and they are clear what's expected of them as well.

Be their life coach

We work hard to put people in control of their own lives, by educating them in how to focus on their life plans, not just the next three months. Ultimately it's all about having willing volunteers working with you.

There are too many corporate victims that go to work for companies and then blame them for everything that's not right in their lives. They forget they have a fundamental choice.

Similarity of spirit, diversity of strengths
We focus on creating what we call high-performing Super Teams, ensuring that we understand the strengths of the people within the team, and then balancing those strengths. The principle of balancing strengths applies to board members and their PAs, too. My bottom three strengths are fairness, harmony and being restorative. My PA's top five strengths include my bottom three. So, she provides my balance and my conscience.

Hire smart people and then challenge them
There is no bigger crime than hiring a smart person and then not stretching them. The Number One reason people used to leave Microsoft was that their job wasn't stretching or challenging enough, closely followed by the fact that they didn't like their manager.

Employee engagement, not satisfaction
It is not our job to make employees happy or satisfied. It's our role to ensure they are engaged; engaged in where the company is going, and the role they can play to help Microsoft achieve its vision, whilst at the same time developing their own career.

Ensure every employee can answer these three questions
1 What are the three things that you are paid to do?
2 What are your strengths, and your USP (Unique Selling Point)? If you left the company and came back as a consultant, what would we pay you to do?
3 What motivates you, and what does reward to you look and feel like?

Source: Stephen Harvey, Director of People and Culture, Microsoft UK. Steve used this formula, which should be familiar if you know the work of Marcus Buckingham of Gallup, to lead Microsoft UK to the Number One spot in the UK 2003 Great Places to Work survey.

(Being) good is good for business

So, leading attentively is part of the foundation of being an inspired leader. The core theme of this chapter is the need to recover permission to lead when the reputation of business and business leadership has been eroded by a series of high-profile corporate governance issues. Which means that as well as being attentive, you also need to deal with the whole issue of being 'good' (not to be confused with being nice).

Business used to be whatever you could get away with. That's no longer the case. Because you can't get away with it. There's now overwhelming evidence that greed at the top can seriously damage an organization's reputation and, consequently, its ability to perform in the marketplace. The *zeitgeist* – the spirit of the age – has shifted noticeably since the 1980s. Then, the business context was summed up by Gordon Gekko in the movie *Wall Street*:

> **'Greed is Good.'**

Greed was the great motivator. 'Get rich quick' was an aspiration, not a sneer. Personal greed at the top used to be an expression of muscular capitalism; a coded indication of the health of an organization ('Wow: have you seen how much they can afford to pay their CEO?'). Now, instead of a badge of honour, or the purest distillation of capitalism, CEO demands for fatcat pay, apparently regardless of company performance, are now suspect. The message it gives out is this: if you're motivated by personal greed, how far will you go to expand and hang onto your pile; as far as Enron? As far as Worldcom?

The myth that the highest-paid business leaders achieve the best results is just that; a myth. The CEO of Northwest Airlines, Richard Anderson, earned almost $3 million in 2002, 126.3% up on 2001, despite declining passenger revenues, thousands of layoffs and substantial wage cuts for those further down the hierarchy. Herb Kelleher, chairman of Southwest Airlines, claimed just $320,000 in salary for the same period, then waived a quarter of that because of the financial turmoil that hit the airline industry after 9/11. Southwest has been (and still is) the most consistently profitable airline in US history. Its stock market valuation is worth more than the rest of America's top ten airlines put together, including Northwest.[4]

After the bursting of the dotcom bubble and the corporate excesses of the late 1990s, 'Greed is Good' seems as dated as the loud ties and platinum cufflinks that went with it. Good, it seems, is now good for business. Personal restraint among leaders at the top is now back in fashion. But, it's a battle that's still being fought out as we write this. We are seeing the skirmishing in shareholder revolts against excessive boardroom compensation packages on both sides of the Atlantic.

The law of reciprocity

Don Peppers, one of our members (he of 1 to 1 fame[5]), has been developing his customer thinking into the realm of ethics as part of this whole issue of re-establishing legitimacy post-Enron and obtaining the permission you need to do business and to lead.

Don points out that one almost unintentional spin-off of leading an organization that is premised on furthering the interests of its employees, associates and customers is that you find it is automatically ethical and self-policing. You can't have one (people and customer focus) without the other (ethical behaviour). In an argument that parallels and further develops the Harvard 'Service Profit Chain' work of Heskett *et al.* in the 1990s,[6] Don has researched some of the most profitable organizations in the US and the UK and reported back to us that their very profitability is linked to their determination to represent the customer's interest rather than their own.

It used to be an unwritten law that the basis of the relationship between supplier and customer was adversarial. You had different, indeed, divergent interests. You were two economic forces pulling in opposite directions. It was a tug-of-war. Your interest as a supplier was in delivering as little as possible for as high a price as possible. The customer's interest was the exact opposite.

The relationship was a classic one of negotiation, as with employers and employees. The adversarial nature of the relationship was fuelled by asymmetrical information: suppliers could make money simply by knowing more than their customers, and withholding information (that there was a better deal down the road). The inflated profit margins of the financial services industry over the past few decades are based entirely on customer ignorance. As we get closer to perfect information – well, a whole lot more comparative information, anyway – that kind of information advantage disappears.

The dynamics have shifted. Don Peppers puts it this way: 'When is the customer going to enter into the maximum possible value exchange with you? When they trust you to act in their interest'. Same goes for your employees, of course. One of the most successful direct writing insurance outfits in America is USAA. Their annual renewal or retention rate runs at 98%. 'They treat their customer, explicitly, as they would want to be treated themselves if they were the customer. That's at the core of how they do business. It's the old human law of reciprocity, of recognition that the other is worthy of respect. It's as true of your leadership as of your customer relations: there is no separation here; one feeds directly through to the other', says Don.

We love the recipe of Dee Hock, the founder of Visa, for applying the law of reciprocity to inspired leadership. It goes like this:

PhD in leadership (short course)

1. Make a list of all things done to you that you abhorred.
2. DON'T DO THEM TO OTHERS. EVER.
3. Make another list of things done to you that you loved.
4. DO THEM TO OTHERS. ALWAYS.

Dee Hock, founder of VISA[7]

Don's contention is that the law of reciprocity is so powerful that if you ingrain employee and customer trust as an integral part of your corporate DNA then you are inherently an ethical company. The ethics part comes in here: 'Imagine how hard it would be in that kind of company for a rogue CFO to try setting up Tyco-style shenanigans', says Don. 'Corporate antibodies would emerge to prevent it'. Here are Don's personal leader guidelines on how to be good:

How to be Good

Not all ethical issues are clear-cut. Legal rules are based on actions – 'doing something' is legal or not. Ethical rules are based on intention, and intention is invisible. So, Don Peppers proposes four principles to help keep our organizations straight. These are his personal rules for de-greying ethical issues. You may want to use different ones in your own organization. Use them to stimulate debate and surface what is and what is not accepted ethical behaviour.

1. Full disclosure
Anything that can be exposed to the light of day without anyone being ashamed or embarrassed, that's ethical. But, it does not follow that the converse is true: just because you keep secrets doesn't mean they are unethical. Deception is an acceptable part of business when practised against the competition.

2. Aiding and abetting
If someone else benefits from an unethical act and you take no action, you're just as guilty. You have to have a culture where people, in effect, will police each other if they think the customers' or other stakeholders' interests are being compromised.

3. Fiduciary responsibility
You don't act alone, but as a member of your organization, representing the interests of your stakeholders. You don't skew the company's actions to suit your own personal moral view. If there is too much of a gap between the two, quit.

4. Level playing field
George Orwell said: 'The difference between capitalism and communism is that capitalism is dog eat dog, whereas communism is the other way around.' The only reason for tolerating capitalism and free markets is if everyone is given an equal chance. Any decision not to give equal opportunity due to prejudice is hypocrisy.
These four principles should be applied to any business trying to earn its customers' and employees' trust.[8]

Your mother wouldn't like it

Or you could use Sir Nick Scheele of Ford's simple test: don't let anyone do anything that your mother wouldn't like. 'I've been through thousands of hours of budget meetings, poring over the financial dealings of our company, and I've never yet come across something that my mother wouldn't like. And that's a damn good test to apply. If you are the kind of leader that sails your organization up to the limits of what's allowable, chances are you and your people will cross that line sometimes, probably inadvertently,' Sir Nick told us.

From CSR to CSO

Business tolerates 'responsibility'. It complies with it. And compliance is big business now, a veritable career path in the making that has grown like Topsy following the perception of corporate scandal and the consequent need to manage risk and reputation more thoroughly. The banks and other large organizations have 'compliance officers' sprouting up all over to police what has to be done and pronounce when the *de minimis* legal limit of responsibility has been met. Inspiring it isn't.

Business complies with its responsibilities. But it seizes opportunities. The relatively unpopulated area beyond compliance is the land where competitive advantage is. This is about seizing opportunities and using them to create distinctive organizations that people want to buy from, work for and invest in because it makes them feel good to do so. Large organizations emphasize their Corporate Social Responsibility, or CSR, practices. The most inspired leaders tend to see the agenda as Corporate Social Opportunity, or CSO. As David Grayson,[9] a leading light in the emerging CSO field, says: 'You can no longer tag this stuff onto your organization with a launch, a lunch and a logo. Responsible business has to be engrained in the fabric of the organization.'

Leaders of older companies who lack the sense of authenticity and of being a values-led business that inspires many people today (as in young inspiring companies like Virgin & Southwest Airlines) have had to acquire it by attaching themselves to good causes – cause-related marketing and all that stuff. At its worst, a corporate giant attaching itself to a warm and fuzzy good cause has all the appeal of the proverbial lipstick on a pig.

But, if it's done with integrity, the pig can start to look quite attractive. Marjorie Thompson, who used to head up Saatchi & Saatchi's cause-related marketing unit, has researched a number of examples of big business successfully following Professor Gary Hamel's injunction to get a cause, not a business, by borrowing someone else's (cause, that is).

Inspiring causes

Procter & Gamble, for example, created a brand in South Africa by getting together with Save The Children. Called 'A Better Start', the brand went from zero to 17% consumer brand awareness in seven weeks. Not bad for a tired old mature company. The mobile phone network Omnitel says its mission is to improve the world. You can subscribe to its text message service to find out how clean the beach is that you are planning to visit. The medium (the cellular network) isn't in itself 'good'. It's by aligning itself with the causes that its users are charged up about that it becomes seen as good.

You can go deeper. Fashion is, literally, superficial; all about surface. But Liz Claiborne, the $3.7 billion leading US fashion house, has run an eleven-year campaign against relationship violence. Not a one-week or one-off *pro bono* activity; an eleven-year campaign that gives it a deeper purpose and a stronger relationship with its customers than the competition.

Firing employees up

Research carried out by the Corporate Citizenship Company shows that employees are far more highly motivated about working for a company with a good social record than one whose purpose is only making money. It's measurable. British Gas found the same thing when it surveyed its call agents. P&G harnessed this need for higher purpose by introducing a programme that allowed some interns to spend nine months working for the World Health Organization in Africa.

'There is a relatively little-known piece of research that was done by a small change management consultancy in the summer of 2001,' says David Grayson. 'They went to a number of leading organizations like Goldman Sachs and the *Financial Times*. They interviewed people identified as being the most talented in their organizations. They asked them: "What are the important things for you in your choice of organization to work for?" Of course, the usual things about reward and recognition and the opportunities afforded by an interesting job and growth came up. And of course there were some for whom the mating call of the Porsche remained the most important driving force. But, they were surprised by a significant number of people talking about what they call the 'dinner party effect' or the 'halo effect'. Am I proud to talk about who I work for when I'm out Friday night or at a dinner party? Can I identify with the organization to which I am expected to give a great amount of loyalty and commitment?'

Naïve and innocent?
We are also seeing the emergence of young brands that explicitly trade on the brand values of being straightforward and honest. Virgin is the obvious one. Innocent Drinks, the UK's market-leading 'smoothie' producer, is another. Its co-founder, Richard Reed, one of our members, says that the purity that is the selling point of the product – its all-natural ingredients – has to be expressed in everything they do as an organization.

He interprets that as transparency, plain business dealings and communicating with a sense of humour – being po-faced about 'innocence' is counter-productive; it comes across as pious. Innocent is a great example of an organization that satisfies the hunger for authenticity that runs through this chapter as a connecting theme.

Here are Richard's tips for how to harness what we might call anti-marketing – being transparent, natural and honest. These tips apply as much to a leader's communication internally as to external marketing.

How to be Innocent

Innocent *what*?

Innocent is the UK market leader in 'smoothie' and 'thickie' drinks. Innocent's products are stocked in 3,500 outlets, from Harrods to the Priory de-tox centre to an oil rig off the coast of Scotland where they are delivered every day by helicopter.

Innocent's ten-year business plan was accomplished in four years, achieving a turnover approaching £11 million (around $20 million at current exchange rates) in 2003. It has picked up a string of awards in the process, including the Orange Small Business Award and Ernst & Young's 'Best New Entrepreneurs'. Innocent was even described by the Millennium judges, when looking for innovations that defined the 21st century, as 'a new brand which encompasses the spirit of the millennium'.

So, how does a company that basically crushes and bottles juice become so distinctive? Eight lessons distilled from Innocent co-founder Richard Reed:

1. Own a tone

Innocent speaks in an understated, ironic, wised-up language that is a form of anti-marketing in a marketing-saturated age. Its HQ in Shepherd's Bush, London, is called Fruit Towers. Consumers are hungry for this kind of authenticity and self-deprecating humour in place of hype. One word sums it up – natural, like the company's products. The tone is unwavering and instantly recognizable. A poster on the London Underground shows a big picture of an Innocent smoothie bottle and the words 'List of contents: Fruit … There, that was boring, wasn't it.'

2. Seduce your customers (and employees)

Read the Innocent bottle labels to see how you can seduce your customers virtually for free. It's a stressful world. People warm to you if you are playful and make them smile. One Innocent label includes this product information: 'Separation may occur (but mummy still loves daddy)'.

Look closely at the embossed lettering on the bottom of the plastic smoothie bottles and you find messages such as 'cut bottle in half to make kayaks for two hamsters' or 'replace lid before reading this'. Innocent discovered the bottlers would emboss any message they like at no extra charge. What messages would your company have chosen?

3. Keep the main thing the main thing (SUC leadership)

Keep centred on that Single, Unifying Concept that focuses and defines everything that you do. For Innocent, it's pure and unadulterated drinks that taste good and do you good. The unmet need was the UK government's 'Five a Day' guidance for consumption of fresh fruit and vegetables, previously an impossible target. Now, consumers who can afford the £2 premium price can achieve their daily recommended fruit intake with one small Innocent bottle.

Longaberger in the US is the extreme example of focus that inspires the people at Innocent. 'We use it as an example when we are inducting people. It's the market leader in making picnic baskets and so its company HQ in Ohio is designed as … a giant picnic basket built on the edge of a lake.' Do a Google image search for it: it's an incredible sight; a giant picnic basket that, when you peer at the picture closely, has windows in the sides and is clearly ten stories or more tall.

4. Care

… or at least have a motivation beyond cash. Consumers and employees today respond most to integrity and passion.

5. Worry about reality, not image

'My previous work was in an ad agency and was all about finding out what people wanted, and making them associate what they wanted with the brand being advertised. But, consumers (and employees are consumers, too) have evolved and grown filters that screen out the average of 3,000 marketing messages a day we all receive. Be REAL and they'll love you for it.'

6. Make it easy for people to make friends with you

Be open and encourage feedback wherever you can. Innocent learnt from Birmingham & Midshires Building Society. On its website is a 'phone a boss' button. Click on it and pictures of the senior management team pop up with their direct line and home phone numbers.

7. Be consistent

Innocent's kookie tone extends to its delivery vehicles. The cow bus that delivers its thickies has horns, a tail and a 'moo' button on the dashboard. Its 'grass' van is covered with fields of undulating grass that people come up to and stroke when it is used at promotional events. 'At the Glastonbury rock festival they didn't just stroke it, they tried to smoke it …'

8. Do sweat the small stuff

The lids on Innocent's drinks say 'Enjoy by …' instead of 'Use by …'. Lesson? Deploy every means at your disposal to express your corporate personality, your distinctiveness. From airlines to PCs, the basics now all work to such standards that it is the details that decide whether you're hot or not. It's the ice creams handed out during the in-flight movie and the massage in the Club Room that make a Virgin Atlantic rather than a BA. Compared with the price of running a 747, how much is an ice cream?

Source: Richard Reed, co-founder Innocent Drinks

Of course, a large number of high-performing organizations and their leaders don't come with a CSR-type halo around them, nor do they appear to be innocent and playful. They have a reputation for ruthlessness, taking no prisoners, for playing hardball with their suppliers and even their customers. Their power of attraction is not based on being perceived as nice people to do business with. Nobody would accuse, say, Rupert Murdoch, of being anything less than ruthless and News International of being anything less than highly-driven.

But Murdoch easily qualifies as an inspired leader who achieves extraordinary results, albeit a leader with clear dynastic tendencies. He is true to himself. And he leads a highly-entrepreneurial organization that is made in his image and that has an inspired approach to risk, allowing its leaders at all levels to take chances and fail (but not too often …) as the inevitable price of sector-changing business innovation.

Being inspired is not necessarily about being nice. It's about the T word. As the one-word taglines for those Budweiser commercials tell us, the one thing employees, customers and the rest of your stakeholders want in a world of spin is to know they can trust you as a leader whose word is

True.

This chapter drew on the thinking and practices of the following Inspired Leaders Network members and friends:

Al Gosling

CEO, The Extreme Group of Companies. Al is one of the most authentic leaders we know. He runs a group of eight extreme sports-related companies. The Extreme brand is one of the eight most powerful in world sport, up there with Manchester United and the Olympic rings. 'The only suits we wear in the office are wetsuits … and flip-flops,' says Al.

Charles Dunstone

CEO, Carphone Warehouse. Charles uses the movie 'Pay It Forward' to help engrain the interests of others as a driving force in his organization's culture.

David Firth

David helps organizations achieve creative change and is co-author of *Corporate Voodoo* and author of *The Corporate Fool*.

Chris Lorimer

Head of Service Development, Barclays Bank.

Professor Aidan Halligan

Deputy Chief Medical Officer, UK Department of Health.

Simon Woodroffe

Founder, YO! Sushi

Seth Godin

Marketing pathfinder and author of *Permission Marketing*.

Dorothy Mackenzie

Founder, Dragon, which helps organizations integrate Corporate Social Responsibility into how they do business.

Dan Germain

Fridge magnate (sic) Innocent Drinks. Dan is in charge of Innocent's kookie tone of voice.

Richard Reed
Co-founder, Innocent Drinks.

Stephen Harvey
Director of People and Culture, Microsoft UK.

Don Peppers
Founding partner, Peppers & Rogers.

Sir Nick Scheele
President & COO, Ford.

Julian Stainton
CEO, Western Provident Association.

Mark Sismey-Durrant
CEO, Heritable Bank.

Marjorie Thompson
Founder C3i, former head of Saatchi & Saatchi's cause-related marketing unit in the UK and former chair of CND (the Campaign for Nuclear Disarmament).

Ellis Watson
General Manager, Mirror Group Newspapers and Chairman of the Newspaper Publishers' Association in the UK. Ellis was a marketing director at News International under Rupert Murdoch and the guy who made *Who Wants To Be A Millionaire* the most successful TV format of all time when he was MD of Celador, which produced it.

David Grayson CBE
Director, Business in The Community.

They have to want to follow you

This chapter in 30 seconds

Increasingly, people are seen as your one source of sustainable advantage: welcome to the age of human capital. Yet systems for dealing with people are mainly control systems derived from the machine age, when your capital didn't have a mind of its own.

The existing work contract isn't rich enough to engage your people's hearts and minds. So, re-invent it. Expand the meaning of work. You need an employee value proposition, an 'EVP'. And you need to set a shared context; inspired leaders are storytellers.

Re-recruit constantly. To engage your people's energy and talents whole-heartedly, you need a 'TGIM' working culture.

Many organizations find their human resource is led as if it were an orchestra. But, they actually need a jazz band. Or a bit of rock 'n' roll. Inspired leaders know that talent is resistant to an industrial model of control. The answer is to kill the boss … and reincarnate yourself as head coach.

They have to want to follow you

> 'I joined Virgin because I wanted rock 'n' roll. I wanted the big challenge, the big job, the big car, but I wanted rock 'n' roll as well!'
>
> *Finance director of a Virgin Group company*

Why should anyone want to work for you? Or 'with you' as CNN founder Ted Turner used to say. 'You don't work *for* me, you work *with* me!' he would reputedly bellow at employees he met in the elevator if they gave the wrong answer to the question: 'And what do you do?' At least so legend has it. This is a serious question and it is about you as an individual, as a leader, as well as about your organization or department or business unit. Why do people work and why should they want to work for, or with, you in particular?

Before you get too far down the list of perks, pay, parking space, free coffee, comfy chairs, your sunny personality and ability to motivate, here's possibly the most successful job advertisement in the history of recruitment:

> 'Men wanted for hazardous journey. Small wages. Bitter cold. Long hours of complete darkness. Constant danger. Safe return doubtful. Honour and recognition in the event of success.'

It was the advert placed by Shackleton for his Antarctic expedition of 1915. Our Network member, Professor Aidan Halligan, likes to show it to his colleagues in the National Health Service. 'I often show this to our staff and say: "I think that's the reason a lot of us joined the NHS". And they laugh out loud. And that's when you know you've connected with them.'

In the 2000s, we aren't necessarily any less materialistic than we were in the greedy 1980s. But, for many in the developed world, most of what we traditionally aspired to materially – the reason our parents and their parents went to work – has been achieved.[1] The rest is just excess. And, deep down, we know it. As the surrealist comedian Steven Wright says:

> **'You can't have everything …**
> **Where would you put it?'**

The anti-work movement

If we just worked to feed and clothe ourselves and to keep a roof over our heads, a large proportion of people living in developed economies could achieve their basic needs by working one day a week. Thoreau famously worked out that he could live by doing paid work for just a few days a year, an experiment that involved living in the woods and roasting the occasional rat. We wouldn't recommend it. The point we are spiralling in towards is clear, and you don't need to refer to a Maslow-type hierarchy of needs to appreciate it: attitudes to work are changing.

These are plate-tectonic-level forces we are talking about here. People are increasingly questioning the unquestionable: whether they have to or indeed want to be full-time employees any more. The rise of individualism, most notably since the 1980s, has contributed to the growth of anti-corporatism, of a reluctance to be a salaryman or woman. Choice has entered the arena of work.

Increasingly, your best workers are volunteers. It's up to you to keep them working for you, to re-recruit them constantly, if you like. Because, they could easily work with someone else if they found that more interesting, more rewarding or less stressful. Or they could choose to spend less time working and pursue other passions instead. There are powerful forces at

work here (or, more precisely, in reaction to work, rather than at work); forces that simply didn't exist ten or twenty years ago, and you have to set up your own power of attraction to counter them.[2]

Free me!

You can see evidence of the growing reluctance to be employed all around you: in downshifting; in your best people deciding they don't want to be corporate beings and leaving to set up for themselves. In the UK you can see it in the mass exodus of people moving to start a new life abroad, growing olives or running ski chalets, using capital released from their overpriced UK homes.[3] Everywhere you look, people are exploring alternatives to the inadequacy of meaning and lack of control inherent in much modern work. Increasingly, talented and thoughtful people don't want to be employees. They want to be owners, free agents, portfolio workers – something more autonomous, more in control, than an employee.

The need to be in control of your own life is one of the most powerful forces in the universe. The partial answer is to give people ownership of their work. Here's Henry Stewart, one of our members, explaining how to do it:

How to set your people free

Happy Computers is a 40-person IT training company with a £2 million turnover. When I started it in my back bedroom, I was convinced I was a great trainer and my job was to grow a company of people just like me. So, I would watch my colleagues train and then give them feedback; what I thought was good, what was bad. You can imagine how well that went down.

I soon learnt that you can only create a second class copy of yourself if you manage using yourself as a model. At Happy Computers now there are no managers, only co-ordinators. What you want to aim for is for people to feel they own their own job.

Henry's job ownership model

1   Set the principles.
2   Set the targets.

3 Step back and let them perform, any way they like, as long as it's within the principles and hits the targets.

4 Your job is support.

It's very different from the ISO process-type methods I began with.

Your prime role as a people manager is …

People work best when they feel good about themselves. So, what's your role as their manager? Exactly. Yet, how many people manage that way?

Mistakes are compulsory

At Happy Computers, you are expected to make mistakes.

When Microsoft set up their new research institute in Cambridge in the UK, the head of the centre was told: 'If every one of your projects succeeds, you will have failed'. Think about it. Exactly: no stretch, no fail. It's the same for your front line. They should be free to experiment within the principles and targets.

Don't design for the worst

As Branson said: 'Never set up a system on the assumption people will do it wrong. Expect people to perform at their best.'

Split yourself in two

It's a common assumption in business that the person who is best at making business decisions is the person who is best at managing people. In our experience, the two rarely go together. I no longer coach anyone at Happy Computers because the business decided it was not my strength. So the decision-maker and coach can be different people, and often should be.

You are not there to give approval

Any passing upward of work for approval before the work can continue or a decision can be made restricts people's creativity and slows you down. So, minimize approval levels. If you can, make your approval role redundant.

Henry Stewart, founder, Happy Computers[4]

Work is life

In developed countries, where, as we have established, the basic needs of many people are met by working a day or two a week, work becomes part of a wider search for meaning and fulfilment. Instead of 'work to live', people want to mesh work into their lives. It's not about achieving work/life balance. Work snakes in and out of our lives so much that trying to define life as the things that we do outside work is now seriously outdated. Companies that acknowledge the need for work/life balance are buying into a myth.

The widely-accepted concept of 'work/life balance' assumes three things:

1   work is a bad thing;
2   life outside work is a good thing; and
3   the two are divisible.

All three of those assumptions are wrong.

This is just an inaccurate way of thinking, based on outmoded industrial models of work, and smart leaders don't buy into it. Many of the people working the longest hours in this long hours culture aren't forced to. They are the best paid. More than half of them say they choose to do it because they like it. Richard Reeves, a leading authority on the changing nature of work, points out that some studies show that working long hours is an effect, not a cause of dissatisfaction with life outside work. The broader point here is that work *is* now life. The barriers are down. The big question – the meaning of life – has a little brother now: 'Since a large chunk of my life is spent working, what's the meaning of work?'

Make meaning

Inspired leaders anticipate and respond to this need for higher meaning by re-inventing work, by humanizing the organization to a degree. Take this, from the Virgin Group of companies' website:

'Our companies are part of a family rather than a hierarchy. They are empowered to run their own affairs, yet other companies help one another, and solutions to problems come from all kinds of

sources. In a sense we are a community, with shared ideas, values, interests and goals. The proof of our success is real and tangible.'

Work as a community of like-minded people, as a family, as a community of interest. This re-definition of what work is and of the relationship between an organization and the people who work for it is a common factor when you look closely at how the workplaces of inspired leaders differ from those of ordinary leaders. Simon Woodroffe, founder of Yo! Sushi, found his inspiration in a work of fiction: 'Arthur Conan Doyle's *The White Company*, about a band of people who travel around, bound together by common values … that always appealed to me as a far more attractive kind of 'company', far above the common meaning of the word today, as applied to corporations. That's the kind of thing I always wanted to create and be part of – I never wanted to be employed.'

The sensible question that arises out of this whole re-examination of what work is, is this, of course: What's your role as a leader now, then? Partly it's the communication of meaning – helping to answer the 'what are we here for?' question. In traditional communities, there has always been the storyteller, usually a village or tribal elder, who interprets events and gives them a framework of meaning. Stories are how meaning is communicated. As we have established, people are looking for more meaning in work, and your leadership role therefore becomes something of a storyteller.[5] At corporate level, organizations suffer from trying to tell stories that are too similar to each other, or that lack integrity of meaning; hence the proliferation of sound-alike vision and mission statements and strategy confusions – strategy is just a story grandly told.

Meaning and conversation

To state the obvious, storytelling requires communication skills. Inspired leaders are great communicators. And, before you break out in a cold sweat as so many leaders do, since communication is often their weak point; communication *can* be learned. However, leadership communication too often means, in the mind of a leader, the ability to persuade, convince and win people over to the leader's point of view. We see this particularly in politics. Ask a political leader to explain the unpopularity of a policy they are wedded to and they will answer that they need to work harder to convince the electorate; to win the argument. As a rider, they'll probably blame the media for distorting the whole issue. In fact, genuine shared meaning, rather than an imposed agenda, comes from conversation.

Having said that, if you can't string a few sentences together without confusing people, you'll never make a great leader. Yes, we all have two ears and one mouth, but what comes out of that mouth has to be easy to understand or people will just tune out and start thinking about what they're going to have for dinner tonight, all the while nodding and looking for all the world as if they are absolutely with you on this one.

All is not lost for the tongue-tied leader. We can give you an example here from Sir Nick Scheele, Ford's Chief Operating Officer, to demonstrate that there are techniques you can learn from other leaders to create an effective communications toolkit if you weren't born with one yourself. Later in this chapter we deal with the widely-ignored part of leadership communication – listening to others (the conversation thing mentioned above). Sir Nick's point, here, is about getting your message across so it is remembered:

Three is a magic number

'In leadership communication, don't underestimate the power of three,' Sir Nick told us. 'I can only remember three or so objectives for a period of time, so I assume our people are wired the same way. It helps achieve a sharp focus when you are engaged in a turnaround, or channelling energies into targets.

'For example, to focus any group of people, you need to communicate a vision, expectation and set of measures (note the magic three). When we came up with our turnaround strategy at Ford of Europe, we took all 1500 middle managers from across Europe to Badeneuer in Germany, in two shifts, and ran them through our vision, including why we were closing Dagenham, the UK HQ which they thought was our birthplace (note: sometimes leaders have to re-write the corporate story). We made clear the expectation: that they were crucial to delivering on the vision; that it was in their hands. We targeted them on three things (the magic three at work again): tripling productivity, taking $1K of cost per car out of the cost base and re-energizing the distribution network.

'Incidentally, it's common in internal corporate communication – particularly informal or unofficial communication – to erode morale without intending to. The scapegoating of middle managers is a case in point. When I joined Ford I found they were referred to as "the layer of clay". How motivated and energized would you feel if you knew that's the kind of language the people at the top were using to refer to you and your peers?'

Sir Nick's instinctive reliance on segmenting communication into three bites is sound. People find it easier to retain communication that is broken into chunks of three. Amazon was the first to apply this principle to making web navigation easy by breaking all its customer-facing processes down into three. 'As easy as 1,2,3', 'As simple as A,B,C'. It works: try it as a framework for improving your leadership communication.

Context is king

Remember the dotcom mantra: 'Content is king'? Turns out they got a letter wrong. In business today, context is king. A grander phrase for creating meaning by storytelling is creating and communicating a shared context. Most organizations have at least two contexts: employer and employee. To achieve a high-performing organization, you need first to set up a shared context, in which 'them and us' is replaced by one genuine shared vision and purpose. Shared meaning is a powerful thing. Tracy Goss, in her book *The Last Word on Power: Executive Re-Invention for Leaders Who Must Make The Impossible Happen* defines context as 'the human environment that determines the limitations of your actions and the scope of the results your actions can produce.' Goss says 'the context is decisive. This explains why copying someone else's strategy – while it may improve your reputation – never seems to lead to effective action and never leads to making the impossible happen.'

See Chapter 1 *The Last Word on Power: Executive Re-Invention for Leaders Who Must Make the Impossible Happen* (Tracy Goss, Pub. Doubleday Currency 1995), for more information and specific leadership and organizational examples of 'the context is decisive'.

Mike Harris, founding CEO of the world's first telephone-only bank First Direct, and currently vice-chairman of Egg, goes so far as to say, 'In my experience, management development is a waste of time. Context is all, and it is in the leader's hands.'

So, the inspired leader is a storyteller, or – if you feel more comfortable with this – a creator of shared context. At Southwest Airlines, ask any employee what business they are in and they won't say, 'the airline business'. They'll say, 'the freedom business'. Because Southwest's mission is to democratize the skies, to allow people to fly who would not have been able to visit family and friends by air without Southwest's low prices.

You extend that context down to individual job level by allowing people to see how the output of their work contributes to the company's overall goals. Remember that old story about John F. Kennedy touring NASA headquarters and stopping to chat to a worker with a broom? 'And what do you do?' asked the President. The man, a janitor, replied, 'I'm helping to send a man to the moon, sir.'

I made this!

As well as a common cause, a shared context, a compelling (and authentic) story around which people can coalesce, the business drivers installed by great leaders are designed at least partly to provide challenges for talent that will make them want to stay. For example, Stuart Hornery, the CEO of Lend Lease says: 'Every project we take on starts with a question: "How can we do what's never been done before?',[6] because Hornery knows, that is the mindset that will attract the creative talent that gives his extraordinary company an ongoing competitive advantage.

Some go even further and allow the context to be created by the people who work for the organization. Gerry Farrelly, Director of Training at the UK Midlands company Farrelly Facilities & Engineering, has been attracting international press attention for the way his company made a stand – or set up a shared context – that his people didn't just buy into, but developed themselves. Actually, the press coverage focused mainly on TV news images of Gerry hugging his workers at the door as they came into work in the morning (which aired as far afield as Japan). Gerry tells us his people set up the stunt to symbolize how different his style of leadership was.

Gerry says that in the late 1990s he noticed that his people – like himself – simply weren't happy with their work. 'I said to them: "I'm taking a year to work out a new way of being. I'm fed up with a constant, low-level dissatisfaction with my life and work. I'll keep you all informed as to how it's going. And you can come with me on the journey, if you like … "'

And they did. Gerry defined his journey as 'to introduce fun, enjoyment, empowerment and leadership from the bottom'. The target was to turn the enterprise into what Farrelly employees call a Happiness-Centred Business. That doesn't mean life at Farrelly's is one long party with no-one getting any work done: happiness as party-time is what happens when you define life as something that happens outside work; 'work hard, play hard' assumes that working hard can't be enjoyable, so you have to play just as hard to make up for it.

Gerry didn't look outside himself as the start point for changing his culture and the people who work for him. He did the Gandhi thing: 'Be the change you want to see'. He took the lead. He also had the inspiration to realize that you don't instruct people to join you. You don't impose change on others while remaining inviolably the same yourself. Inspired leaders *invite* their people to join them on their journey.

Here's an extract from a company handbook written up (significantly) by Farrelly's workforce themselves to describe the new culture they created. Note the refreshingly human nature of the language as opposed to the corporate-speak most brochures adopt:[7]

The Truth: We tell the TRUTH to each other and to our customers and suppliers. The whole story, not just part of it. We don't stretch it, bend it, or avoid it. We say it as it is.
Vision: We are striving towards a 'peak performance organization'! Farrelly Facilities & Engineering Ltd wants to work with and for like-minded people, so that we all achieve our primary aims.

Training: Training is a clear signal that we believe in tomorrow. We have no fear of training people and them then leaving. Our greater fear is not training them and having them stay. There is something we know about you that you may not know about yourself. You have within you more resources of energy than have ever been tapped, more talent than has ever been exploited. Let's get started.

Commitment: We make a commitment to ourselves and our clients to deliver world-class and legendary service. When we make a commitment we keep it, and we will move mountains to make things happen. Lack of commitment allows people to blame others and duck the real issues. We should all feel a sense of responsibility to achieve commitment in each other.

IQ versus EQ: Make no mistake, IQ is important, but without Emotional Intelligence we cannot deliver world-class service. Our talent and heroes need these six basic attributes: empathy, social skills, motivation, self-regulation, self-awareness and emotional skills. These skills will allow our performance to be outstanding, because you will demonstrate in your actions how much you care.

Individualization: We don't say 'everyone is treated the same' because at Farrelly Facilities & Engineering Ltd you are treated as an individual, our people and our clients. We nurture all our people, listening to their needs and expectations and use words like love, fun, lust and funky to express ourselves. This is our strong belief: that our approach offers extraordinary results in both people and the company's performance.

How inspiring is that language! And, as Churchill said, get the passion right and the rest will follow. Farrelly's 'stand' is based on ancient Chinese philosophy – the Tao Te Ching – an unlikely but apparently effective rallying point for bringing people together as champions of a common cause, of a shared context.

'To be an exceptional business, your people must have the desire and drive to do it right and do it now. At Farrelly we achieve this by encouraging each individual to think and act as a profit centre and marketing engine,' says Gerry.

That's how they achieve happiness: not by letting people take it easy and removing pressure, but by reconciling the human with the corporate. It seems to be working: the company's turnover doubled in three years and its employees now describe themselves in the company handbook (written by them, not the management, remember) as 'among the happiest on this planet'. Farrelly's business is air conditioning and facilities management. So, even an unglamorous sector can be pumped full of passion by the right kind of leadership.

Keep off the bus

Farrelly's success in enrolling people in a cause that they define and describe themselves is in stark contrast to the standard approach of defining a cause from on high and trying to rally people to the flag to engage their energy, align their efforts, and thereby create a high-performing culture. As Aidan Halligan says, you can't injunct motivation and harness it to your plan. Motivation is intrinsic.

Uninspired leaders go on roadshows around their constituencies, present their vision at mass company meetings and invite everyone to 'get on the bus'. Puh-lease! So, that makes your colleagues passengers, sitting there twiddling their thumbs while you take them where you say they want to go. This isn't inspiration: it's ego, bandstanding and lip service. Organizationally, it's top-down and manipulative and the best you'll get out of it is a lot of people nodding, eating the prawn sandwiches and then getting back to work as usual once the roadshow has passed through. It's why the abiding response in most organizations to top-down change initiatives is one of cynicism. Like buses, there'll be another one along in a minute.

If you want some kind of step-change in your people and your organization's performance, then rallying the troops Boss-style won't cut it. Inspired leaders kill any Boss tendencies in themselves and develop their coaching abilities instead. If you're open to change yourself (and if you're not, then you're not an inspired leader), then this change is equivalent to a caterpillar into butterfly metamorphosis. You have to kill off one stage before you can move to the other. Here's one of our members on how to kill your Boss tendencies:

Kill the Boss: Seif Saghri on how to morph from Boss to Coach

You don't wake up great

Anyone who is great at what they do didn't get there alone. You need someone to unlock that greatness, whether you're a violinist or a tennis player. Andre Agassi doesn't need someone to teach him to play tennis. But, he has a coach. So, how do you become a coach?

Adjust your character

Adjust your character may seem an odd thing to say. But, I had to do it. Bosses are dead. Coaches are it. You have to make a conscious adjustment to be a coach not a boss. Here are ten steps:

1   Put your ego in your pocket.
2   They're people, so are you. So, be personal: even hug, if it's appropriate.
3   Publicly admit your mistakes.
4   Get yourself off the pedestal.
5   Get rid of the 'employee' mentality.
6   Be fair.
7   Treat people like you want to be treated.
8   Show three things: Trust, Respect, Appreciation.
9   Meet people: get out there and talk.
10 Listen, ask, give feedback.

Your role is

- Encourage challenges to the status quo.
- See problems as breakthrough opportunities, not causes for blame.
- Teach 'The Way' and 'Excellence'.
- Encourage people to take risks. You unlock talent by letting it take risk.

As Napoleon said: 'The art of government is not allowing men to grow old in their jobs'.

Communication binds your company together

The Coach is your one-to-one role. Leveraging the best from everyone as a group demands constant communication. That's the fabric of any company that holds it together.

Communication tools
You can never have too much communication. Here are some of the tools we use:
- 'Hey, Seif' suggestion and good deeds box.
- Quarterly meetings followed by fun gatherings.
- News: business and personal; what's going on with the company and personal news about the people in it.

Emotion in the workplace
Business is personal. The distinction between the two is false. Acknowledge emotion at work. Here are a few ways we generate emotion and enthusiasm:
- We blow a horn every time someone makes a sale.
- We run competitions.
- Offer on the spot bonuses.
- Regular awards given publicly.
- Special company events planned by management, not passed to someone else to arrange.

From employer to concierge
Work and life blur together. Acknowledge this, don't fight it. Remove the tension between the two wherever possible. For example:
1 We allow people to make their own hours.
2 Let them know they can attend school sports' days because it's important, and make it clear you trust them to make the time up.
3 Remove executive perks. We have none.
4 Recognize hardship proactively: if someone's been on a two week sales trip abroad, make them take a couple of days to recover.
5 If people are working ten hours a day for you, small, cheap things like providing a dropping-off point for dry-cleaning can help recognize the blur between work and life.

Seif's three-point conclusion
1 Put your employees first (above customers).
2 Treat them as your most valuable asset (don't just say it; show it). Small gestures send big signals.
3 Business is personal. Get the emotional stuff right.

Source: Network member Seif Saghri is CEO of Motivano.

Now, what we've heard from Happy Henry, Seif at Motivano, Gerry Farrelly, Mike Harris and other inspired leaders quoted in this chapter so far, is in stark contrast to the way most large organizations and their leaders work. In classically run, large organizations, people play to music that has been written for them (processes), take the lead from the conductor (the boss), respect the hierarchy and know their place. Problems tend to be 'official'. The board, or its problem sub-committee, decide 'this is a problem' and people are called together to solve it, often with a pre-prepared process.

Orchestral failures

Top-down exhortations to 'be more innovative', 'act like entrepreneurs' 'be more dynamic' and similar decrees from above are designed to galvanize performance levels to achieve the breakthroughs, turnarounds, step changes and all the other ambitious targets facing you today. But, they nearly always fail. There are more cases of failure than success in trying to change an organization's culture to catch a supposed new wave of opportunity. Trying to jump from temporary monopoly to temporary monopoly, rapidly adapting your organization to be ready for the next leap, as the authors of *Funky Business* describe,[2] has proved a hard trick to carry off for the Vivendis and Marconis of this world.

The barriers that large organization change initiatives run up against are largely systemic: how you recruit, train and performance manage your people. If you recruited an orchestra, you won't get them to play like a jazz band. Change programmes and management training will tweak changes, but the key to fundamental change comes back to this, once again: change the context. Research at Shell Internet Works, for example, showed that to galvanize people dramatically, Shell had to change remuneration, recruitment and performance measurement systems to give employees a context in which they could be more dynamic. Shell, in effect, re-wrote their part in the story for these employees, giving them a more meaningful context. More on this below. First, a bit more about how your jazz band organization should look and feel.

Thought is money

Woody Allen, himself an accomplished jazz clarinettist (well, it helps sustain the analogy, doesn't it), famously said that most of life is just about showing up. Maybe it was in classical organizations, where you had to fill a particular chair in the orchestra. But, work is not about just being there any more. Physically being at work 9–5 misses the point. The new currency of work for knowledge workers is *thought,* and that happens anywhere, and to its own rhythm; on the bus, in the bath. Thought is money, not time. IT has eroded the boundary between home and work. Stupid leaders don't get this and continue to alienate people by trying to stop personal use of IT at work, assuming time spent at the desk is where work happens. But, if your people are getting the job done, so what?

'Virtual workplaces will drive managers crazy. They no longer have arbitrary control, and that means so much to organization men', said Jon Johnson the American professor of management.[8] Give people control over their time and trust them. It will pay back. In many contexts, you can safely dispense with working hours. Time works differently in jazz band organizations. In classical organizations, it's like a symphony: you know when it begins and finishes (9 to 5, Monday to Friday, everyone stopping

© 2004 Ted Goff

"I don't have time to write performance reviews, so I'll just criticize you in public from time to time."

and starting together). But, as we've established, regulated time of that kind is no longer the unit of currency of work. Stop treating employees as if it is and you will have made a crucial break with an outmoded way of thinking about work and your relationship with your employees. You are no longer in the business of buying time from people. You're in the re-recruiting business.

Re-recruiting people, or igniting their passion for the first time if your organization has never had any, demands far richer and more nuanced conversations than most old-style managers are used to, both when dealing with people collectively and individually. Most FTSE companies carry out an employee attitude survey once a year. It can take four months to analyze and report on the survey. If you're a manufacturer, you monitor your machinery in real-time. So, when it comes to taking the pulse of your most important asset – all the big companies say human capital is their biggest asset – why do you do it sixteen months in arrears? You are not measuring the present. You are measuring how that asset was performing sixteen months ago.

Leaders ask smart questions

There is an old saying: If you want to know the strategy, ask the generals. If you want information, ask the troops. If you are stuck in the rut of annual employee attitude surveys, you are not finding out what is really going on now. You have to engage with your workforce constantly if you want them to be engaged. The same principle applies here as with your corporate communication to those outside the company: increasingly, people don't want to be broadcast to. To develop a level of engagement in your employees requires a dialogue, a conversation. In many cases, that means the dominant 'voice' (as the grammar teachers at school used to put it) that you need to adopt as a leader is no longer the 'vocative' or instructive voice; it's interrogatory. Bosses issue instructions, commands, orders, declarations. Leaders ask smart questions.

At Microsoft they ask questions like: 'On a scale up to 5, do you get to do the great work you are capable of each day?' Cisco has its famous 1–5 feedback scale for everything – from induction training to corporate broadcast speeches delivered by the top man on everyone's desktop, Cisco employees have the same rating scale sitting in the corner of their screen as their customers. It's a form of constant polling: the aggregated feedback clicks tell the organization if a training module needs to be withdrawn and re-worked or if Cisco CEO John Chambers needs to update his talking-head 'welcome to the world of Cisco' video that greets new hires on their desktop, because the existing one isn't scoring too well.

Captain Mike Abrashoff, the legendary leader of the battleship *USS Benfold*, used to ask his crew these three questions every six weeks:

1   What do you like about working here?
2   What don't you like about working here?
3   If you were the Captain, what would you change?[9]

Segment your people

No, not as in dismembering. That's old-style leadership. Today's employees work best with all limbs intact. Frank Douglas, VP at Shell, and a member of our Network, has pioneered the concept of segmenting your Employee Value Proposition, just as CRM practitioners segment their customer base and proposition. Frank discovered not one but four workforces at his company and crafted four EVPs[10] to meet their different needs. The categories range from 'free agents in residence' to entrepreneurs, builders and career seekers, each of whom have different characteristics, risk appetites and motivators.

So, to retain your talent, your Employee Value Proposition needs to vary according to the employee type you are appealing to. Your workforce may obviously segment into different types from Shell's. The core point here is that Frank discovered what his people needed in an EVP through a conversation, by asking them and acting on their responses. He started off by developing an overarching EVP for Shell Internet Works when he was HR Director there. 'We asked our people *"What are your aspirations from work?"* The result is our Employee Value Proposition, which became Shell Internet Works' signature', says Frank. The five elements of this EVP, defined by the employees themselves, remember, were:

1   inspired Leadership;
2   high calibre and engaging peers;
3   challenging and exacting work;
4   share of success; and
5   global reach and exposure.

For an EVP to work, like a Customer Value Proposition, you need to pay far more than lip service to it. Shell defined these five propositions and then enshrined them in its contract with employees. To fulfil point 4 of the EVP – a share of success – Frank had to revamp the whole pay system, and that took five months' negotiation with the board. It was disruptive but necessary to embed that within the EVP, because Shell Internet Works was about inventing and developing new businesses.

Then Frank and his people customized the EVP to fit the four types of worker they had defined – again, just as you have to customize offerings to customers.

Shell Internet Works' customized EVPs

1   Free Agents In Residence

Characteristics: Little loyalty. Change jobs frequently. Get rich quick.
Risk appetite: High.
The EVP: Very high salary for short project or large upside potential for longer engagement. Compact, self-contained job description.

2   Entrepreneurs

Characteristics: Control and decision-making. Need to influence company direction. Wealth through IPO. Feeling of ownership.
Risk appetite: Lower than Free Agents. Higher than Builders.
The EVP: Attracted to small startups/great ideas. Create/lead/play critical role in senior management team. High upside potential.

3   Builders

Characteristics: Excited by challenge. Need to influence company direction. Control and decision-making.
Risk appetite: Lower than Entrepreneurs. Higher than Career Seekers.
The EVP: Relative autonomy. High-level decision-making and leadership. Tough challenge.

4   Career Seekers

Characteristics: Professional development. Room to grow in company. Job security.
Risk appetite: Low.
The EVP: Exciting job. Opportunity to grow.

The unavoidable conclusion from all this listening and crafting of EVPs is this; inspired leaders actually take their lead from their people when it comes to getting their buy-in.

This chapter drew on the thinking and practice of the following Inspired Leaders Network members:

Robert Levering

Co-founder, The Great Place To Work Institute. With Milton Moskowitz, Robert researches those 'Great Place to Work' lists to work in America, Europe, the UK and so on, published by *Fortune*, the *FT* and others.

Richard Reeves

A *Management Today* columnist, Richard is described by the *Guardian* newspaper as 'Britain's leading expert on workplace trends'. He is the author of *Happy Mondays*.

Don Tapscott

Don is President of New Paradigm Learning Corporation and a digital guru.

Stephen Harvey

VP, People and Culture, Microsoft UK. Stephen is that rarest of things, a finance director turned HR director. 'They call me the Antichrist of HR and I'm proud of it', he says. Stephen took Microsoft UK to Number 1 in the 2003 UK Great Place to Work survey. Since contributing to this book, Stephen has moved on to become Managing Director of Goldsmith's the jewellers.

Frank Douglas

Frank is currently HR VP for Shell's exploration division. Interesting anecdote: Frank, who trained as a trumpeter in a former life at the Juilliard School, the New York academy featured in the movie *Fame*, is the only HR director we know to have been invited to speak to the Queen's Household about culture change. He recalls this exchange:

Sir Michael Peat, Prince Charles's Private Secretary, asked:
Q: 'What is the quickest way to change a culture?'
A: 'Change the leader', fired back Frank ('It was a flip answer', says Frank).
'I'll tell the Queen that tomorrow,' replied Sir Michael drily.

Professor Aidan Halligan

Professor Aidan Halligan was appointed Deputy Chief Medical Officer for England in January 2003. He is also the Director of Clinical Governance for the National Health Service. He is still a practising obstetrician (though only on occasional days). When Prime Minister Tony Blair asked Aidan to scale up the patient-centered improvements he had helped lead at Leicester Royal Infirmary, and replicate those radical changes across the 1.1 million employees and hundreds of Trusts that make up the NHS, Aidan replied, 'OK. What do you want me to do in year 2?'

Henry Stewart

Known as 'Happy Henry' by his colleagues, Henry Stewart is founder of the radically different IT training company Happy Computers, which won the 2003 *Management Today*/Unisys Service Excellence Award (UK Overall Winner). He also wears incredibly loud shirts. Henry is the only leader we know who can claim to have successfully deployed the leadership techniques of the radical South American entrepreneur Ricardo Semler.

Wendy Thomson

Wendy works at Number 10 Downing Street, where she runs the UK Prime Minister's Unit on Public Services Reform. Originally a North American academic specializing in urban transformational change techniques, Wendy became a practitioner. When she was CEO of Newham, a local authority in inner east London, Wendy and her top management team spent Saturday mornings out on the streets asking local people how they felt about their borough council and how they would like it to be, as a reality check to keep the 'top people' grounded. It was a 'meet the Boss' morning. The local people were the Boss.

Simon Woodroffe

Founder, YO! Sushi, the restaurants where food is served on conveyor belts and drinks are served by robot waiters who shout, 'Get your fat **** out of the way! Some of us are trying to work around here!' if they bump into you. Simon is busy launching an empire of YO! Everything Else, including luxury capsule hotels (Yotels!) and a knowledge transfer company called YO!How. He also recently recorded an album with The Blockheads, Ian Dury's old band, including a version of his own song 'How I found my YO!'

Seif Saghri

CEO, Motivano, which provides a range of web-based HR tools and employee benefit solutions to inspire people to want to work for their company. More than 1 million employees on both sides of the Atlantic use Motivano's services.

Sir Nick Scheele

COO & President, Ford Motor Company, respected as one of the business world's most inspiring leaders.

Larissa Joy

COO, Webber Shandwick UK. Larissa was named a Global Leader of Tomorrow by the World Economic Forum at Davos, class of 2003. Larissa was recently put in charge of a merger between two companies, whose people subsequently refused to talk to each other. She took the 'culture development' budget designed to knit them together as a single team by climbing mountains and crossing rivers, and instead used it to open a temporary free evening bar where people from the two organizations could meet and get to know each other. It broke the ice.

Tracy Goss

Tracy is an internationally recognized consultant, author and lecturer and one of the foremost authorities on Organizational and Executive Re-Invention. President of Goss Reid Associates, Inc, a management consulting firm based in Austin, Texas she specializes in bringing her Re-Invention Methodology to visionary leaders and their senior executives working in partnership with them to invent and strategically plan an "impossible future"; and to re-invent themselves and their organizations to successfully lead their industry into that future

Mike Harris
Founding CEO, First Direct Bank. Executive Vice-Chairman, Egg.

Gerry Farrelly
Director of Training & Creatology, Farrelly Facilities & Engineering.

Make a difference

This chapter in 30 seconds

Speculate to accumulate? Nah, too risky. Innovate to accumulate. Different is harder to beat than better. But, innovation is less about new ideas than you might think. Copying across sectors to create difference can be innovation, too. 'New to you' we call it.

Ideation is the easy part. Monetizing the ideas is the tough part. You achieve that by building an innovation machine. You'll need a funnel and some gates. Avoid premature evaluation.

Innovation is, by definition, unpredictable. That means accepting mistakes and building containment zones to limit the damage.

Think big. Start small. Scale fast. Unstiffen: Let your hair down. It is in the successful balance between chaos and order that innovation thrives.

Irritation is part of the process. Mavericks are a pain to lead. But, they are the grit that delivers the pearl. They will challenge you at every turn. Get used to it. You no longer lead the making of products or services. Your job is to make a difference. Literally.

SECRET 4

Make a difference

> 'We still use these old warfare metaphors for business leadership, quoting ancient Chinese generals and applying them to business. But "beat the enemy" doesn't work. You need to compete to be unique, not to be the best.'
>
> *Professor Michael Porter, in an interview with one of the authors*
>
> 'You do not want to be the best of the best. You want to be considered the only ones who do what you do.'
>
> *Jerry Garcia, The Grateful Dead*

If you are going somewhere you've already been, you don't need inspired leadership; everyone already knows where it is and what it looks like. If you are going into uncharted territory – and that, by definition, is where innovation lives – then you have to have inspired leadership to get you there. Management is about predictable results. Leadership is about an apparent paradox – planning for unpredictable results. If you want to be a little bit better, stick with management. If you know that the only way to compete is to be radically different, then you've opted for leadership whether you like it or not.

Evo or revo?

The conceit of course is that this is an either/or thing. Those who advocate Big Innovation, like the consultant Tom Peters, deride small-scale incremental improvement. If you are focusing on many small improvements continuously, you can't blow the whole thing up and invent something completely new, they argue. Clayton Christensen maintains that the innovator's dilemma is this: sustaining and developing existing offerings stops you from jumping to disruptive new ideas that may transform your market.[1]

Evolution vs Revolution is usually the way the two approaches are characterized. The Evolutionists, with their fiddly little improvements ('Let's make that knob a teensy-weensy bit bigger in the next model. Careful, though; don't want to give anyone a heart attack or anything …') are presented as timid Sunday drivers on a sensible trip out in their Morris Minors – those ones with the neat indicators that pop out from the side like a little flag – only to be splattered across the tarmac by a passing Toyota Landcruiser, barrelling down the highway so fast it doesn't even notice the squelchy bump as it passes over them.

The truth is that you need both; continuous improvement of your existing ways of working, plus a constant awareness of where the Next Big Thing will be coming from and a readiness to grab it as it flies past, so it can take you with it. If you're really inspired, you'll be the one driving the NBT as it flashes past.[2] But, you'll be continuously improving it as you go. That's the funny thing about innovation: it's never finished. Big Innovation and continuous Small Innovations should be able to live happily together without one rolling over too quickly and squashing the other.

Surpetition

The new primacy of *different* over *better* is simple: the supply-side of the economy is overcrowded. You know this stuff. As the economists have always told us, everything heads towards commoditization. Only it has never happened this fast before. We have gone beyond competition to 'surpetition', a phrase coined by lateral thinker Edward De Bono. Linear competition – competing on the same racetrack of benchmarking, the pursuit of best practice, product quality, ISO 9000, customer service initiatives, excellence programme etc. and tedious etc. – is operational improvement disguised as strategy; the stuff of management. 21st century leaders need to recognize this and make a stand for boldness. We repeat: not instead of, but as well as.

To get better at leading innovation you need to seek out emergent practice that is being pioneered and proven by leaders who are ahead of their time. So, where do you find that kind of leadership? At the margins, on the edge of your vision, in the wild lands that are characterized as maverick business practices. If you don't believe us, try Jack Welch, the most radical big business leader there has been in recent years (despite his political conservatism):

> **'You can't behave in a calm, rational manner. You've got to be out there on the lunatic fringe.'**
>
> *Jack Welch*

In a phone interview with one of the authors, the strategist Gary Hamel told us a great story to illustrate the fact that innovation lives in wild places. He explained how Nokia morphed from a maker of gumboots and toilet roll holders into the market leader in portable phones, by sending its drab Finnish engineers to live for six months among the *fashionistas* of London's King's Road, the tech-loving young generation of central Tokyo's nightclub set and the trend-setting dudes of Venice Beach, California. 'Soak up how these people live, then come back and invent for that future', they were told. Nokia went out looking for the unevenly distributed future and found it. Or at least found enough clues to invent the rest themselves.

The essential tension

Note the essential tension in the Nokia example between experience (Nokia's engineers) and novelty (the edgy environment and future-defining consumers they surrounded themselves with). 'The essential tension' is Thomas Kuhn's phrase. Kuhn is the scientific innovator's guru.

Abigail Tierney, whose doctoral research included work on how Nobel laureates use leadership to achieve their exalted results, says Kuhn's insights on innovation are exactly applicable to business, too: 'The assumption that there is an automatic connection between youth or novelty or freshness and successful breakthrough innovation is too simple. A lot of investors made that mistake with the youthful dotcoms in the 1990s. Most Nobel prizewinners in science are recognized for breakthrough findings in their 50s. But they were invariably surrounded by a team of people who brought enthusiasm and freshness to the task at hand. Leadership is about a degree of humility in knowing you need other people around you to get the answers. And successful innovation springs not just from youth or novelty, or the previously unthought thought, but from an essential tension between experience and freshness.'

Innovation thinking focuses too much on the search for novelty and not enough on the other half of the essential tension – using the traditional structures and ways of getting things done to change those very ways of getting things done. Too often the innovation gets trampled underfoot by the elephant, by the existing culture and processes, when what you really want is to position innovation at the elephant's shoulder, whispering in its ear. 'For innovation to succeed you need the entrepreneurial spirit, but you also need people who understand the traditions of the organization and ways to get things done, so you can change the organization from within. Real geniuses embody both', says Abigail, who divides her time between IBM and being a research fellow at the Said Business School, Oxford University.

17 ways to kill a new idea

Well, we can't all be geniuses. But, as Abigail points out, the idea that innovation comes from a lone genius inventor – the Thomas Edison archetype (which Edison himself did not fit and never claimed to) – gives inspired leaders a get-out: surround yourself with a team that is committed to innovation, the way Nobel scientists do. Not changing, when surrounded by a sea of change, is dangerous. The alternative path is innovation that constantly feeds the bottom line: that's what you want and you know you want it. Oh, but there's a problem. It's the baggage that comes with the experience side of the essential tension and that too often tips the scales away from successful innovation. It's another word that begins with an 'I'. And, like Kryptonite is to Superman, *inertia* is innovation's nemesis. It'll destroy your innovation efforts faster than you can scream 'Help me; I'm melting!' unless you destroy it first.

The problem is that inertia is the most powerful force in the universe.[3] Or at least in your organization. Probably. Most organizations, despite their rhetoric, are difficult places in which to introduce and develop ideas for changing how you work. One of our members was running a workshop on change and tried this experiment to illustrate the power of inertia: he asked the participants to switch seats after the coffee break. They wouldn't, because they were comfortable where they were, thank you very much.

'A new idea is delicate. It can be killed by a sneer or a yawn; it can be stabbed to death by a joke, or worried to death by a frown on the right person's brow,' said Charles Brower.

This email on how to kill a new idea, doing the rounds of the Net, highlights symptoms of the inertia disease. Any of them sound familiar?

1   See it coming and quickly change the subject.
2   Ignore it. Dead silence intimidates all but the most enthusiastic.
3   Feign interest but do nothing about it. This at least prevents the originator from taking it elsewhere.
4   Scorn it. 'You're joking, of course.' Make sure to get your comment in before the idea is fully explained.
5   Laugh it off. 'Ho, ho, ho, that's a good one. You must have been awake all night thinking that up.'
6   Praise it to death. By the time you have expounded its merits for five minutes everyone will hate it.
7   Mention that it has never been tried before. If the idea is genuinely original, this is certain to be true. Alternatively, say, 'If the idea's so wonderful, why hasn't someone else already tried it?'
8   Say, 'Oh, we've tried that before' – even if it is not true. Particularly effective with newcomers. It makes them realize what complete outsiders they are.
9   Come up with a competitive idea. This can be dangerous tactic, however, as you might still be left with an idea to follow up.
10   Stall it with either of the following: 'We're not ready for it yet, but in the fullness of time.' 'Let's wait until the new organization has settled down.'

11 Modify it out of existence. This is elegant. You seem to be help-
    ing the idea along, just changing it a bit here and there. By the
    time the originator realizes what's happening, the idea is dead.

12 Try to chip bits off it. If you fiddle with an idea long enough,
    it may fall to pieces.

13 Make a strong personal attack on the originator. By the time
    he or she has recovered, the idea won't seem so important.

14 Appoint a committee to sit on the idea. As Sir Barnett Cox
    observed: 'A committee is a cul-de-sac down which ideas are
    lured, then quietly strangled.'

15 Drown it in cold water. As in: 'We haven't got the staff to do
    it … the intangible risks would be too great … that's all very
    well in theory, but in real life …'

16 Return it to sender with: 'You need to be much more specific
    about your proposal.'

17 If all fails, encourage the originator to look for a better idea.
    Usually a discouraging quest. If he or she actually returns with
    one, start them looking for a better job.

Ideation is not innovation

There's a lot been written about innovation as the creation of ideas,
focusing on how to develop an ideas culture that helps break down
the forces of inertia. Kris Murrin and her colleagues at the creativity consultancy ?What If! have collected a whole toolkit of methods for how not to kill ideas. 'Some companies have developed
their own structure to support the suspension of judgement. For
example, Southwest Airlines' University Of People is an official
"no zinger" zone,' say Kris and her colleagues in their book *Sticky
Wisdom*,[4] by way of example. 'Zingers' is Southwest parlance for
undermining, critical or judgemental comments.

There are plenty of innovation consultancies and books focusing
on creativity as the front-end of innovation. *Sticky Wisdom* is probably one of the best of them (and we're not saying that just because
Kris, one of its authors, is a member of our Network or because
we share a publisher: honest).[5] There are workshops galore on
changing your hats, river jumping, even 'improv management'
– adapting improvization as practised by stand-up comedians,[6] all

designed to increase the rate of ideation among your people; to encourage and equip them to come up with new ideas for how you do your business. OK, do all that, but don't think that's all there is to innovation. It's just the start.

Think '1 in a 1,000'

At the risk of sounding completely perverse, we have to say that innovation is not, in fact, mainly about coming up with new ideas. Apple's graphical operating system is widely assumed to beat the pants off Microsoft's Windows. And to have, ahem, inspired it. Yet which one is dominant? As an idea, Sony's Betamax VCR format was simply better than VHS. Better picture quality in a visual medium equals 'bound to be a winner', no? Apparently not. Success is clearly not about the primacy of ideas. The game goes to the best developer and adapter of ideas, the best and fastest killer of ideas that won't work, the best exploiter of ideas that will.

Ideation is just the front end of the innovation process. Proportional to its importance, ideation is like the 5% of an iceberg that is visible.[7] It gets all the attention, but it's the 95% under water that is where all the dangerous stuff is. Coming up with new ideas is relatively easy compared with what you have to put them through next. Developing those ideas into moneymaking propositions is the hard bit. Leo Roodhart of Shell GameChanger describes post-ideation development as the 'valley of death'. Shell calculates that for every thousand ideas generated, one becomes a profit-making business idea, while the other 999 have to be killed off. The one in a thousand rule is a pretty good rule of thumb. We're talking here about BIG business-changing ideas.

New to you

By contrast with the widespread emphasis on innovation as the creation of ideas out of the blue, we would argue that adopting 'New to You' processes and practices that have been proved in other sectors is the innovator's approach to innovation. Remember our quote from posthumous honorary member Pablo Picasso? *Good art-*

ists copy. Great artists steal. Adapting innovations from other sectors reduces risk. And it increases the chances of consumer acceptance, because the consumer is familiar with how the concept works.

The benefits of drive-thru check-in for Virgin's First Class passengers were instantly understood because customers knew what a drive-thru was already. Virgin Atlantic can swipe ideas from outside because that was part of its culture from the outset. Branson made a point of hiring from outside the airline industry when starting up the company to distance himself from established practice. 'We are not in the airline industry,' was his famous phrase. 'We are still in the entertainment industry, only at 30,000 feet.'

To get you started on New to You innovation, here is our four-point framework for becoming a master thief, for perfecting the art of innovation through cross-sectoral ideas theft:

How to steal ideas from other sectors and transplant them into yours

Our four-step guide

1 *Take the moral high ground.* When you encounter resistance from older hands who know better, use 'Why don't we start from the customer's standpoint?' Nobody can argue against that. It's code for 'Give me some consumer research, not sectoral jargon.' And then test market it. Jump over the heads of the people who have 'always done it this way' and appeal to a higher authority – the customer.

2 *Avoid the technical trap.* People who are entrenched in an industry's practices usually default to a technical solution instead of a customer-focused solution, because established practices tend to be from a supplier-led era. An example from British Airways: the Edinburgh shuttle had just touched down at London's Heathrow and was urgently needed elsewhere, to replace a plane that had been taken out of service. Those in charge came up with a solution that worked, technically – taxi the aircraft over to the area where it was needed and disembark the passengers there.

This was the fastest solution for turning the plane around. But, the plane was full of Club Class passengers who would have had to wait an extra twenty-five minutes for the manoeuvre to be carried out – adding 50% to the 50 minute flight time. As a technical solution it was fine, but it would have alienated a planeful of BA's best customers.

Think lateral instead of technical: for example, BA went to a yacht manufacturer to design the cabins for its bed-seats, because yacht craftsmen are used to designing luxury into small spaces. It's the opposite of the 'not invented here' syndrome.

3   *Concentrate on people rather than process.* It's a common mistake to attack processes and organizational structure first. But, the first thing you need to change is the mindset of your people. Get them used to thinking, 'How would a car manufacturer have done this?' If you need to change the service paradigm, send them to Marriott or Prêt-à-Manger to learn how. Identify enthusiasts as early as possible, because you will need allies to push against sectoral inertia: you can't do it alone.

4   *Admit what you don't know.* There are people who go into, say the railway industry and make wholesale changes, only to find they've thrown out the baby with the bathwater. It happened at Eurostar (the train service between the UK and continental Europe). A new marketing team was brought in and the old railway experts thrown out wholesale. The new CEO had to bring some of them back later because genuine industry expertise had been lost with them. Don't assume 'Old doesn't work. New does.' Or vice versa, of course.

Look for other sectors with similar problems to your own and ask them how they solve them. You'll be amazed at how ready they are to share with you. British Airways had a problem with waiting times at one of its Heathrow terminals. They looked around and decided Disney were the masters of queue management. So, BA visited Disney and adapted what they do in a theme park to an airport environment.

Source: Network member Hamish Taylor is the man we bow down to at the Inspired Leaders Network as the master of cross-sectoral ideas theft. Hamish is the perfect example of the new breed of sector-hopping leader who has no qualms about taking proven ideas from one sector and grafting them on to create something new in the sector he moves into.[8]

As a caveat here we should say that adapting an accepted innovation from another sector is just one approach, not an exclusive solution to the 'how to lead innovation' question. You sometimes need to take the opposite tack and *not* go for a familiar reference hook on which to hang your innovation. What do you mean, we're being contradictory? Of course we are: inspired leaders spend much of their time running hell for leather in one direction, turning on a dime, then running hell for leather the other way. If you're not comfortable with paradox, you're reading the wrong book.

One of us once interviewed Virgin Atlantic CEO Steve Ridgway, and he pointed out that sometimes you have to take a leap of faith into the unknown, even when your consumer research tells you not to. When Virgin set up its Clubhouse lounge at London's Heathrow airport, research among customers into having a ski machine, toy train set and a famous brand hair salon in the lounge bombed. Customers said they didn't want these things. They obviously understood how they worked, so the lack of a reference point wasn't the issue. They just couldn't imagine it as part of an airport experience. Virgin went ahead anyway. And those funky and continuously-evolving experiences – now extended to in-flight massage in First Class – are part of the defining difference of flying Virgin.

Sometimes you have to go beyond the research, because consumers don't know what's around the corner until you've introduced them to it. And even if you describe it to them in the research, they won't be able to tell you if they would like it because it's too radical for them to get their heads around. Yes, use research to check, but not to generate ideas. Similarly with business-to-business, it makes sense not to listen to what a lot of your existing biggest customers want when looking to develop what you do. Instead, listen to the demands of the small percentage of future-defining customers; those wackos you tend to tune out at the moment. They're a good source of innovation, too.

It's not easy being green

If you're not lucky enough to be a challenger brand like Virgin, but are instead a big, old, challenged brand, then another innovational arrow to add to your quiver is the ability to challenge yourself first. The argument against developing this kind of innovation culture is obvious: expending energy and resources beating yourself up by subverting your own business before the competition can do it seems kind of perverse. Like wearing one of those T-shirts emblazoned with 'Beat me, whip me, spank me'. But, inspired leaders have a streak of masochism.

One of the dominant forms of corporate culture in the 1980s and 1990s was the self-aggrandizing, cult-like status that some American corporations in particular still practise. 'We can do no wrong' was the unwritten loyalty oath. Inspired leaders encourage, by contrast, a more questioning approach, a constant sense of 'we can do this better'. At its extreme you see it in Bill Gates' famous assertion that he assumes Microsoft is at any time maybe months away from being sunk by a competitor that comes up with a staggering innovation; or in Andy Grove of Intel's observation (and book of the same name) that only the paranoid survive. Before the smaller, fleeter, pirate vessels catch up and sink you, runs the logic, you set up a flotilla of pirates inside that develop the ability to beat the buccaneers at their own game.

This is not quite the same as the greenfield approach to innovation. General Motors knew there was a need for a customer-centred carmaker with more flexible and innovative work practices. But, it also knew the weight of its own history prevented it from becoming that new kind of carmaker. So, it set up Saturn as a separate company. Similar thinking applied in the UK when Midland Bank (now HSBC) set up the world's first telephone-only bank, First Direct, and let it build from the ground up. You can argue that both these companies were committed to filling a propositional hole in their existing offering to customers rather than setting up a new form of carmaking and banking respectively that would then supplant the parent. But, hey, it's smart to keep your options covered.

There are downsides to greenfield as an approach to large-scale innovation – cannibalization of your customer base and replication of investment in duplicated functions, for example. Greenfield costs are high and the problem of how to change the legacy culture in the parent company is untouched. But, in both examples mentioned, greenfield has proven to be a powerful way of using radical change to grow your business by raising a kind of mutant sibling, if you will, at a safe enough distance from the original business not to taint the corporate DNA should the experiment go wrong.

The issue is that setting up another company on a greenfield site is a luxury most of us cannot afford, or get the board's backing for. A cheaper alternative is the *Skunk Works* model – allowing your collective band of nutters (sorry, creative mavericks) to set up small units that are allowed to circumvent corporate rules and practise fast-track development of new projects. Skunk Works is the name Lockheed Martin gave to the rule-breaking unit it set up to develop fringe projects that would otherwise have been stifled by the bureaucracy of the organization's rule-bound processes. The skunks got the weirdest ideas to fly – literally, when it came to the stealth bomber. But, since the Skunk Works was originally set up in 1943, this isn't exactly news to you, is it.

Dead bankers walking

The 21st century version of a Skunk Works needs to be more 'of' the organization than cut off from it. You achieve this through a project culture that is comfortable housing experimental bubbles of activity that run alongside the main business of the day. One big UK bank client of ours that will remain nameless is struggling with this whole 'inside or outside' question. It knows its blue chip reputation and stifling hierarchy discourages creative individuals.

The big picture is that the profit pillars of banking are eroding – profits rest on asynchronous information (knowing more than the customer), the time lag involved in transactions, plus the assumption that those closest to the money in corporate mergers and other deals are entitled to a percentage-based slice of it. All of these pillars of banking profit are under pressure. Traditional banking is full of dead men walking. Very well-dressed dead men with Porsches in many cases, it must be said, but you get the point.

At time of writing, our well-known-bank-that-shall-be-nameless has just posted record profits from the usual methods: relying on customer inertia and asynchronous information. Plus some very nice advertising. So, its commitment to changing to more radical ways of doing things is flaky at best. But it knows things will have to change in banking, and so runs a small unit of creative bankers who were originally brought in to develop new forms of dotcom banking before that turned out not to be the Next Big Thing (at least not in the way expected).

'I told them I couldn't work for them any longer because they were so stifling', said one of these mavericks. 'So, they let us set up as a kind of radical generator and developer of ideas as a separate company. Then they brought us back into the fold by buying the company. I guess they'd rather have us inside peeing out than outside peeing in …'

PricewaterhouseCoopers' consulting arm (before they became, briefly, Monday then, more permanently, part of IBM) studied what makes for a non-creative organization and came up with these indicators:

- Prescriptive
- Centralized
- Risk averse
- Hierarchical
- Status conscious
- Low level of vertical communications
- Low level of trust.

Sounds like the typical large organization to us.

The answer is Bubbles

Which is exactly why you need a bubble culture. Delon Dotson, technology pioneer at Netscape and then MP3.com, puts it this way when he's teaching his fellow Network members about how to lead innovation: 'Corporations are in constant stasis. They don't want to move. We try to create a safe bubble, or ring-fence an operation as far away from the corporate middle as possible. If the corporations don't have visionary people at the top then they won't be at the top as corporations. I would get the buy-in of the MD or CEO of the company, get a bubble of people we trust, let them ignore politics and help them do their jobs.'

A bubble sustained by the oxygen of support pumped in from the very top: it's a recurring theme among our more successful members at leading innovation. Gill Cattanach, Commercial Director, UK National Savings, uses the same bubble-speak, independently from Delon: 'We work in bubbles where we take people in from different areas and pick their brains and work out where we want to be and what the vision will be. This is contributing to a major transformation. We have the biggest customer base in the UK in financial services. We will watch and learn, and use the learning to hopefully leapfrog to get to the next space. Although the perception is we are old and fuddy-duddy, you have to change internally before you can change the external.'

Torben Peterson, CIO at Nordea Bank, was a director at Oticon, the Danish hearing-aid maker (hold on: it's much more interesting than that would suggest). Oticon famously morphed itself from a rigid hierarchy into what became known as a spaghetti organization. The slightly anarchic notion of a spaghetti organization subsequently fell out of favour with some analysts of organizational form (who prefer the easier-to-describe, ugh, 'matrix organization'). But, we think there's still a hell of a lot to learn from Oticon's decision to loosen up and encourage tendril-like overlapping connections rather than keeping its people constrained within traditional departmental boundaries.

The way Torben tells it, it was spaghetti or die: 'We had boring products, no marketing and a high cost base. Our solution was radical: to turn the company into a creative organization with two features; firstly, a purely project-based organization, which meant stripping out all the old structure, departments and hierarchy, and secondly, one in which everyone had at least two jobs, to encourage them to move around and see things from a different perspective. We told them at least 20% of their time had to be spent doing something other than their core job.'

Signs and symbols

Oticon centralized its people in an HQ that was designed to hothouse projects: work areas had desks and scientific workbenches mixed together to accommodate project teams. Changing the physical workspace reminds you constantly that what you are doing is different now. It constantly focused people on team-based projects, because that's what the building was laid out to allow. 'It's all about signs and symbols,' says Torben. Oticon even made the mythical paperless office work, something nobody seems to have succeeded in doing since.

'You can touch paper, but only once', staff were told. They are allowed to bring paper into a central paper room. It can only leave that room shredded. 'Scan it there if you want. But, it doesn't leave the room in one piece', is the instruction. A joke suggestion emerged to answer the question, 'What do we do with the shredded paper?' But, the CEO took the joke seriously, approved it, and £100,000 was spent on running a see-through giant pipe through the floor of the paper room, down through the cafeteria to a waste area.

Staff could munch on their open-top sandwiches (it's Denmark, remember) while a relentless cascade of thousands of shredded pages swirled their way surreally past them through the perspex pipe as the centre-piece of the HQ; a moving sculpture that symbolized the way Oticon had torn up its past. Again, signs and symbols have real power.

'That one symbol of what we were doing became the most photographed thing in Denmark', Torben told us. 'The BBC, CNN, everyone came to film it. It made our people feel different about what they were doing. They would read about their workplace in the papers, (before shredding them, presumably) or see it on TV. It made them feel part of something exciting.'

Forcing people to abandon all the old structures and work on target-based projects released their creativity. After a year of restructuring to become project-based, Oticon went on to bring the first fully digital hearing aid to market. Its turnover went up tenfold in ten years to £390 million, with a net income of £80 million. And Torben's share certificates went through the roof; fittingly, since he had sent all that shredded paper through the floor.

Think big, start small, scale fast

So what happens when one of your bubbles produces something with potential, like Oticon's fledgling digital hearing aid? It's here that the metaphor becomes totally mixed up and tortured, because the next stage is for the bubbles to give birth to *pilots*. The pilot is then kind of shown off to the rest of the company, like you would with a new baby. The key to successful pilots can be summed up in six words: *Think big. Start small. Scale fast.*

Start lots of pilots. Pilots minimize the consequence of failure and you can use them to obtain buy-in, by showing the rest of the organization a prototype of your vision in action. A lot of your pilots will fail, even though you put a lot of time, effort and ingenuity into them. That's a good thing. What you decide NOT to do is as important for success as what you decide to do. It is essential to share learning from these mistakes. So, true innovation can only happen in a learning culture. That way, the pilot limits the scope of the damage and then the shared learning stops that error from being repeated.

John Stewart, when CEO of the Woolwich Building Society, cultivated this approach to innovation in what had been a hitherto fairly dull, traditional UK savings institution. It was rather like lighting lots of small fires, but keeping each in a firewalled environment with a fire extinguisher on hand if it turned out to be a mistake. One of the flaming pilots (now there's an image) his people came up with, turned into Open Plan, a new kind of hybrid of mortgage and savings (actually, the Australians invented the offset mortgage first, but that's a different story) that aggregated customers' money into one savings pot, while allowing the customer to manage the money as if it was divided into several jars. This new customer-centred approach was so successful that it attracted the attention of Barclays, who bought the Woolwich to get their hands on it, and made John Deputy CEO of the Barclays Group. He has since moved to head up the Australia National Bank. See: pilots do fly.

Protect mavericks

New to You, bubbles, pilots, challenger brands inside – whichever combination of these innovation methods you put into practice, there is one theme common to all of them: you have to protect your mavericks, even from yourself. Our research shows unanimity on this front among our pathfinding network members. We are told to recruit change agents – non-traditional employees – if we are to transform our companies. But the truth is that you get a hell of a lot of irritation before you get the pearl. As Frank Douglas, HR VP at Shell Exploration, puts it: 'Who wants to manage a rebel? They are a complete pain in the butt. They challenge you. They disagree with you. They break the rules. The usual outcome is that one of you leaves. And, as they are the subordinate, it is usually them. But, the result is that your corporate immune system lives on, having rejected the invader that didn't fit in.' This is Thomas Kuhn's essential tension at its rawest. It's up to you and other leaders to provide air cover for your innovators, protect them from the organization and champion their causes.

So, if you are looking to change your organizational culture; if you are aware of the need to bring in innovation and innovators – change agents who do things differently, mavericks, whatever you want to call them – you have to be prepared for this, get used to being challenged and find ways of accommodating it. Otherwise, any plans you have to change your culture and become faster-moving and more innovative will grind to a complete halt.

Hierarchies and status stifle creativity and persecute mavericks. They value people for what they did yesterday. They imply that the only good ideas come from above. In fact, the best ideas come from junior people challenging you. You have to be a confident leader to encourage this. Hierarchies are a good place for weak leaders to hide from challenges. 'You really have to encourage, welcome and understand loyal opposition', says one of our members, Carolyn Clancy, CEO of Companies House in the UK. Or even disloyal opposition, come to that; if your change agents need to tilt at an authority figure to get their creative juices flowing, and they pick on you, then you just have to be big enough to take it. If it delivers results, then you've done what's required.

Build a difference engine

As well as being about breaking old rules, innovation needs a common set of new rules with which to break the old ones. easyGroup's innovation rules include, for example, that the idea should normally be premised on a significantly lower cost-base than industry incumbents. Stewart Niblock, easyGroup's master of innovation, has worked up his own set of innovation rules, which he shares with us here …

easyGroup's four innovation guidelines
… for breaking into a new market with an innovative business model

1 The existing players have underutilized assets (empty cinema seats, empty plane seats, unrented hire cars)

Only 20% of available cinema seats are sold over the course of a year. Stelios thought: 'It's a fat, lazy industry: just right for us.' Hence the birth of easyCinema with a new proposition for bringing in customers.

2 It normally has to be a price- elastic market

… where easyGroup can change customer behaviour with innovative, flexible pricing. easyCinema's 20p upwards pricing structure, with seats becoming more expensive as the cinema becomes filled, is a case in point.

3 There's scope for outsourcing activity to the customer as a trade-off for low prices

Against complete opposition from his senior managers, Stelios championed the idea that easyCar rental customers would clean the car themselves before returning it if offered an incentive. 'Return it dirty and we charge £10 to clean it. Return it clean and no charge' worked: over 80% are returned clean. Since a significant proportion of car rental staff time is spent cleaning cars, the business benefit of this innovation is obvious.

4 Test it in the marketplace for real

easyCinema's first site, in Milton Keynes, is 500 metres from a successful new multiplex. In fact, the new multiplex is so successful it forced the closure of the cinema that Stelios then bought and re-opened as the first easyCinema. easyCinema re-opened head to head with an established competitor that had killed the predecessor on that site. The only way to test your innovation is to expose it to the real world.

Plus six more guidelines on leading innovation from Stewart Niblock himself

1   Expect the unexpected
Innovation is naturally risky. So don't go into it expecting predictable results.

2   Don't let your funnel become a torture chamber
Every genuinely innovative company has a funnel for processing new ideas. Don't make it a hoop-jumping process with painful layers of decisions. And don't reject ideas too early ('premature evaluation', Sherwood calls it).[9] The tyre company Michelin has a 7-step gate. A new idea has to satisfy each step before it is allowed through the gate into the developmental funnel. But, crucially, if an idea fails at one of the steps, it can be worked on and re-submitted later.

3   Don't ignore your organization's cultural constraints
Inconsistent messages will stifle innovation unless you align the culture. Learn to unlearn and be open about how to tackle personal fear (people are afraid of putting their neck on the line).

4   Innovation doesn't end with the funnel
Once the idea is out in the marketplace you keep on developing it. easyInternet cafes, easyCar and other businesses changed drastically once out in the marketplace. Reality bites. It's painful to admit when your idea needs surgery to make it work. But, it has to be done.

5   Measure and monitor performance
What does success look like? What's the payback time on your innovation investment?

6   And, finally ... two prerequisites for leading innovation
'Unlike cutting costs, or making an acquisition, innovation does not happen just because the Chief Executive wills it. Indeed, it is confoundedly difficult to come up with new ideas year in, year out – especially brilliant ones. Underneath the guru's diagrams, lists and charts, most of the available answers seem to focus on two strengths that are difficult

to create by diktat: a culture that looks for new ideas, and leaders who know which ones to back'.
The Economist, 4 December, 1999

Source: Stewart Niblock, Risk Director, easyGroup. Stewart was Stelios's chief test pilot; the man he gives a new business idea to and says: 'Make that work'. Stewart now oversees strategic risks across the group.

Think the unthinkable

We'd like to finish this chapter with a radical suggestion. Take a look at public sector innovation. There, we said it. Sounds like an oxymoron to our private sector brethren, doesn't it? But behind those grey walls of officialdom, an attempt at bureaucratic *hara-kiri* has been going on since around the turn of the century. Faced with limited resources and a demanding public, governments have been setting impossible targets and urging civil service heads to adopt radical methods to deliver on them.

UK Prime Minister Tony Blair explicitly stated in the late 1990s that he expected his top public service policy people to think the unthinkable. 'Joined-up government' and all those soundbite catch-phrases about creating a faster-moving, more consumer-led form of public service delivery have beneath them a lot of hard work and perspiration. Heads of government departments, hospitals, schools have been looking mighty sweaty lately as they struggle to squeeze out the one per cent inspiration that leads to major breakthroughs.

Wendy Thomson, one of our members, heads a specially created unit in Number 10 called the *Office of Public Service Reform*. Wendy has hosted for us at the Cabinet Office a couple of sessions of a forum we call *The Exchange*, where public and private sector leaders get together to advise each other on how to make change: cross-sectoral pollination is what it's about. Sir Michael Bichard, who headed up the departments of Employment and Education in the late 1990s, neatly summarized the drive behind public sector modernization at one of our Exchange sessions like so: 'In the public sector, we realized we can't tackle engrained social issues by pulling management performance up a few notches. There has to be creativity to achieve breakthroughs.'

The UK's public sector uses a seven-step SPIRALS framework when introducing radical innovation. Here's how it works, including some examples of how the public sector has put the steps into practice in its attempts to deliver on the promise in that injunction to 'think the unthinkable'.

The SPIRALS framework
A seven-step approach to leading innovation

1   Spark generation

Any innovation framework must have a mechanism for igniting sparks – radical ideas that break you out of 'this is the way we have always done this' thinking. De Bono's 6 Hats is an example of a mechanism many organizations have adopted. Stealing ideas from other cultures is another: taking the Maori tradition of restorative justice and transplanting it to the UK, for example, or introducing internal competition in the way NASA did by pitting two teams against each other to come up with the technology to put man on the Moon ... all are examples of ways of generating sparks.

In the public sector, we encourage spark generation by listening to the margins; for example, listening to the hospice movement or the wind power movement can spark new perspectives. One of the greatest innovations in financial services, low cost loans for low income families, came from listening to the Grameen Bank in Bangladesh, from transplanting their principles successfully to cities across Europe. Innovation funding mechanisms are a form of spark generation. For example, public sector staff in the UK can bid from a range of innovation 'pots' to try new ideas.

Combining old things with new things through 'What if?' thinking is another way of generating sparks. What do you get if you put phones and nurses together? NHS Direct, the phone-based medical service. Local authorities have had great success in stopping unruly teenagers hanging around city centres by playing Vivaldi over the public address speaker system.

2   Prototype development

Execution speeds understanding. Again, you need to put funds aside here. The UK government has a £380 million 'invest to save' budget to prove ideas for saving money.

3 Incubation and modification

Every good idea starts out half-baked. It has to. By definition.

We have developed a range of zones (roughly corresponding to government departments such as Health and Education) to incubate innovation, to give ideas space to prove themselves. One example is a project called Working Links, a public-private initiative in the employment innovation zone. It's based in a house in Southwark, South London; looks just like a house, not a government project. The people who run it basically have permission to use their allocated budget any way they like to get people into work. It's incubating an idea that breaks the usual government model of nationally imposed standard 'into work' programmes.

4 Replication and scaling up

You need large scale for successful innovation. Think corner shops and supermarkets. Which are the innovators? Schools are often too small to innovate. So, the Literacy Hour innovation brought in by the government and replicated across all the UK's schools means our 15-year-olds are now more literate than their German or French counterparts. Learn Direct, a remote learning initiative, is another example of a replicated, scaled-up innovation. It now has half a million users.

5 Analysis

Targets, inspection, 'what does this feel like?' experiential analysis and metrics are the cornerstones of our analysis of the impact of innovation. All our management information is made transparent and available on the web (school and police league tables, for example).

6 Learning

… is instilled into all our policy initiatives. We created Talking Heads as a forum for head teachers to exchange learning, where the government doesn't listen in. Honest. In Health, the Cancer Services Collaborative brings together 30,000 people working against cancer at all levels and in all types of organizations. So, you can achieve diagonal slices of people sharing their knowledge and experience that cut through hierarchical tiers and across organizational boundaries. That way we all learn much faster about what works.

7 Space

Close old programmes down to make space and free up money for new things. Unlearn. And give licence to break the rules to achieve the desired end. We introduced a clause to a Schools Education Bill that we copied from a medal given by the Empress Maria Theresa in the 18th century to anyone who had turned the tide of battle by breaking orders. Our equivalent is a clause in the Bill that says any school can do anything that has a demonstrably good chance of improving the education of their children.

Source: Geoff Mulgan, at time of writing Head of the UK Prime Minister's Policy Office.

The main learning point of this chapter is that to lead innovation you need to learn to be like Madonna. No, we don't mean move to London and adopt a Dick Van Dyke 'mockney' accent. We mean be like Madonna as in this comment from Simon Woodroffe, founder of Yo! Sushi:

'You can't create a masterpiece concept anymore and say: "That's it; now we'll roll it out." The 21st century concepts that succeed will be those that continually re-invent themselves, just like Madonna.'[10]

This chapter drew on the thinking and practices of the following members and friends of the Inspired Leaders Network:
Torben Peterson
CIO, Nordea Bank.

Stewart Niblock
Risk Director, easyGroup.

Dr Abigail Tierney
IBM Research Fellow, Said Business School, Oxford University.

Kris Murrin
Director, ?What *If!*

Francesco Zuchelli
IBM. Francesco is the European Foundation for Quality Management's lead expert on innovation.

Gill Cattanach
Commercial Director, National Savings, UK.

Frank Douglas
HR VP, Shell Exploration.

Sir Michael Bichard
Rector, the London Institute, formerly Permanent Secretary at the UK's Department for Education and Employment.

Simon Woodroffe
Founder, Yo! Sushi.

Mike Harris
Executive Vice-Chairman, Egg.

John Stewart
CEO, National Australia Bank.

Delon Dotson
Technology pioneer, Netscape and MP3.com.

Hamish Taylor
Formerly CEO of the Eurostar Group, MD of Sainsbury's Bank and CEO of Vision Consulting. Currently setting up a new airline.

Carolyn Clancy
CEO, Companies House, UK.

Geoff Mulgan
Co-founder of the think tank Demos, Head of the UK Prime Minister's Policy Office (at time of writing. Geoff has since become head of The Institute of Community Studies in East London).

Lead from the edge

This chapter in 30 seconds

It's the Customer Century. Last century was the Supplier Century. The balance of power has shifted. Yet, like generals fighting the last war, most leaders still act as if they are leading a supplier-style 'push' organization.

Leading a customer 'pull' organization demands a different kind of leadership entirely. You have to dismantle push thinking, abandon the assembly line of the mind, learn how to practise post-industrial leadership on the edge instead of at the centre.

Your new relationship with customers is wraparound, not limited to transactions across a supplier-customer divide. It's sensual: based on a distinctive experience that they can see, hear, touch, feel, smell.[1] And it's consensual: complicity rules.

Lead from the edge

> **'We've put the rifle in the hands of the deer.'**
>
> *Fred Newell, author, Loyalty.com*

In 1994 self-styled 'Chief Inspector' Robert Stephens started the
Geek Squad, a computer repair business, with $200 and a bicycle
to take him from job to job in his hometown of Minneapolis. Three
years later, the Associated Press had picked up on what Robert was
doing and wrote this about him:

> **'MINNEAPOLIS – Robert Stephens, the self-proclaimed chief
> inspector of the Geek Squad, has a dream: "The complete and
> total global domination of the computer support business."
> He just might succeed.**
>
> **'Dressed in black slacks, starched white shirt, narrow black clip-
> on tie, white socks and black shoes, Stephens is the founder of the
> Geek Squad, a high-tech company that specializes in computer
> support. From beginning to end, his company is patterned after
> 1960s television police shows, with special homage to *Dragnet*.
> Stephens started alone in 1994, but now employs 12 so-called spe-
> cial agents. All of the agents wear the same uniform as Stephens,
> carry badges and respond to service calls in vintage automobiles,
> the geekier the better. They are on call 24 hours a day, seven days
> a week.**
>
> **'Their motto: "We'll Save Your Ass."**
>
> **'Stephens is not only a *Dragnet* fan, he's a shrewd businessman.
> "It's a military psychosis of a comic proportion," Stephens says
> of a computer crisis. "The humour *not only makes the job fun for***

employees, but relieves the stress for the customer", he says (*author note*: our emphasis).

'And behind the tongue-in-cheek costumes and goofy cars is a business philosophy more rooted in Jiffy Lube than in Microsoft.
'"We're in the fast-food business; quick, small and frequent transactions," Stephens says. "The exotic part of the business is the delivery of the service."
'"We are a living comic book ... and a profitable corporation".'

Chris Tomlinson, Associated Press writer, 1997

That was 1997: twelve special agents. At time of writing, seven years on, there are 700 Geek Squad stores throughout the US and Canada. Robert Stephens has parlayed his bike and $200 into a multi-million dollar turnover business, running a fleet of Volkswagen Beetles decked out to look like black and white cop cars. 'A living comic book ... and a profitable corporation.' What a compelling story. How much more motivated do you think one of his FBI lookalike agents feels when out on a job and interacting with customers, compared with a similarly-aged (20-something at most) IT nerd working for a rival?

Remember the computer genius in the movie Jurassic Park – a socially dysfunctional male slob constantly surrounded by mess and with questionable hygiene habits. IT repair companies struggle to win over the confidence of their customers when the pool of maintenance and repair talent they have to work with comes similarly clothed and with similar habits. Stephens subverts the stereotype, repackaging his people as comic book heroes, disciplined and uniformed, thereby inspiring far more confidence in the customer. At one level, it's an inspired way of getting Generation Y to play corporate.

You can check them out here: http://www.geeksquad.com
So, PC repair can become theatre. Or, in this case, TV-meets-comic-book. What's the significance here for how you lead? Ask a Harley-Davidson senior executive what they sell and you'll get the answer. And it's not motorbikes. 'We sell to 43-year-old accountants the ability to dress in leather, ride through small towns and have people be afraid of them,' says Harley-Davidson VP John

Russell.[2] Customer experiences have replaced products and services.[3] And to lead the creation of customer experiences, you have to learn to walk in your customers' shoes, see the world through their eyes, breathe the same air. Or, in Harley's case, ride the same bikes.

As products become commodities faster than ever before, the 1990s saw the competitive battleground shift to services in many sectors, for both ends of supply chains – business-to-business and business-to-consumer. In B2B, IBM makes more money from services than from selling hardware. In B2C, as Edward De Bono observed, Ford became a bank, making money out of financing loans on its cars.[4]

Not more choice, thanks

Alfred Sloan, the founder of General Motors, brought in product differentiation in the automobile industry and nearly killed off Henry Ford's monoculture of 'any colour you want as long as it's black'. But, in an age of hyper-choice, offering yet more product choice collapses as a differentiator. Customers want a level of control, not necessarily to be overwhelmed with choice.[5]

The 21st century equivalent of Sloan's innovation is a customer experience that takes the hassle out of the customer's life, and shows them some empathy – whether the customer is a multinational outsourcing its IT, or a stressed executive looking for a 15-minute respite disguised as a Starbucks skinny latte. It's less about products and services and more about wraparound experiences. Oh, and a compelling story. Don't forget the story.

Only a handful of leaders get this. Most struggle with defining what a distinctive customer experience even is. If a doughnut can become a unique customer experience,[6] then anything can. The key point most leaders (but not inspired leaders, of course) miss when thinking about 'a customer experience' is the strapline of Pine & Gilmore's 1999 book, *The Experience Economy*. It's this:

> **'Work is theatre and every business a stage'**

Shakespeare was right: all the world's a stage and your business is a collection of players upon it. This is not frivolous. And if you try it at a superficial level, it won't work. Theatre is intense, it's dramatic (by definition), it's emotional – all the things a memorable customer experience should be. Deep theming has deep impact and can even turn a commodity into a desire, as we have seen with the Geek Squad (all the most famous rock bands use them, incidentally, even the Stones and U2. That's how cool the Geeks are). Every step of the way needs to be stage-managed rather than left to the music of chance.

UPS delivery personnel, when carrying a package from their van to a customer, walk fast, with a sense of urgency: they speed-walk. This isn't by chance. A sense of urgency is part of the UPS customer proposition – to always prioritize the urgency of the delivery. So, it has become part of the UPS 'way' to speed-walk when delivering. It's expected. Even walking becomes themed, becomes branded, becomes part of the customer experience.

B2B want experiences, too

If you think this is just for consumers, it's not. It's for business-to-business, too. Our network member Don Peppers tells us how Eneco, the Dutch natural gas supplier, went from selling just gas to managing a complete environment for its business customers. Holland is Europe's major supplier of flowers. They use greenhouses to help grow them. Eneco was supplying the gas that powered the climate control in the greenhouses, but was acutely aware that gas was a commodity and a gas supplier is chosen on price. So it developed climate control expertise, and now monitors and manages temperatures and humidity in its clients' greenhouses. Of course, the clients buy the gas, too. That's not just a shift from a commodity product to a service: it's the creation of a unique customer experience based on the customer's unvoiced needs or wants.

A unique customer experience doesn't have to mean completely re-engineering what you do, though. It's how you do it that makes it memorable in many cases. Here's a particularly creative example from a business-to-business environment:

Wear your customers' shoes?

At St. Luke's, the radical advertising agency based in London, major clients have their own themed room which they can come and work from, whenever they're in the area.

So, meetings with executives from Clarks, the shoemakers, take place in the Clarks room. In typical St. Luke's fashion, the Clarks room is themed around shoes – even the coffee table wears shoes: the legs on the table have feet at the end, which sport Clarks footwear.

How at home do St. Luke's clients feel, do you think? Put yourself in your customers' shoes? The inspired leaders at St. Luke's even put their furniture in their customers' shoes.

Richard Branson calls his group's distinctiveness Virgin Flair. Here's an example of the kind of unique and memorable experience that results from that kind of leadership thinking, from Lyell Strambi, Virgin Atlantic Airways' COO:

I scream, you scream, we all scream for ice cream

Virgin has a number of legendary employees, who epitomize Virgin Flair. One such employee was Sue Rawlings, an in-flight attendant with a larger-than-life personality. People at Virgin still talk about her years after she left the organization. She has become a kind of corporate archetype, an example of 'this is how we behave' that people share through storytelling.

Just before serving the ice cream that Virgin offers to passengers while they are watching the in-flight movie, Sue would duck into the galley, smear ice cream all around her mouth, then emerge and start serving.

As she moved down the cabin she would pronounce very loudly, so that people would look up at her, 'I never touch this stuff myself; I'm watching my weight, but people tell me it's delicious. Enjoy!'

The effect was a wave of laughter that moved down the cabin with her, as passengers looked up from plugging in their headphones or fiddling with the volume control.

And here's an example of creating a distinctive experience even from your call agents, if they have the chutzpah to follow suit (and the existing relationship with the customer to allow it): A customer calling Virgin Money stated very firmly they did not want to be put on hold while waiting for some information. So, the agent sang *New York, New York* down the phone to keep them amused till the information came through.[7]

Remember Richard Reed of Innocent Drinks' comment earlier in this book? When the basics work on a flight, and the planes are essentially all the same, customers' choice could be based on ice cream. Or, in this case, the unique ice cream experience. And how much does an ice cream cost compared with a Boeing 747? The little things are no longer insignificant. The art of the interaction, of the *way* your product or service is delivered, becomes the competitive differentiator, because the product or service is in itself not different enough from the competition.

© 2004 Ted Goff

"I sent all our best employees to investigate our competitor's company, but they never came back."

So, how do you follow suit; how do you lead in a way that delivers your equivalent of a Virgin ice cream experience or in-flight massage?

Tattoo you

Let's strip down how leadership works in Harley-Davidson to help answer that question. The quote we opened this chapter with shows they think and act differently within Harley from the way you might have thought. Yes, they pride themselves on being like their customers. But, the Harley approach to leading the company is less Hell's Angel gang leader than it is Zen and the art of motorcycle manufacturing. Most of Harley's customers are now middle-aged CEOs, lawyers and computer programmers, anyway. But Harley is still possibly the only company in the world whose customers regularly tattoo its logo onto their skin.

We'll hear in a moment from Harley's European MD how leadership translates into that level of customer loyalty. But, first, some staggering figures:

- $10,000 invested in Harley-Davidson in 1986 was worth $1.5 million in 2003.
- Harley's turnover in 2003 was $4.6 billion.
- At time of writing, profit is running at 25% of revenue.
- In 2002 that profit was $1.166 billion.
- Profit growth over the ten years 1993–2003 has been a compound annual rate of 26%.[8]

Harley people use the phrases 'super loyalty' and 'ultra engagement' to explain their success. Here's Harley-Davidson's European VP, John Russell, to explain what they mean:

What Harley-Davidson did to create 'super loyalty' through 'ultra engagement'

'We don't actually *create* loyalty. Our customers give us their loyalty. It's their choice. They choose to show they have a belief in us and in the way we run our business and processes. Most companies see 'brand' as some connectivity to a badge. Harley goes far beyond that. The customer experience is the brand.

'At Harley-Davidson, employees drive processes to create what we call *Ultra Loyalty* or *Super Engagement*. Employees are empowered to engage with customers on a day-to-day basis and constantly find out what they need to do to meet customer needs, then do it! People inside a company are capable of achieving the most extraordinary things for, say, their family and religion. The key to the concept of employees looking after customers is to unlock that.

'Some say "It's OK for Harley: the product is so exciting." But, these principles can be applied to any company producing anything: paint or nails; it doesn't matter. The knowledge you need is all in your front line. That is where the 'trust zone' with your customers is, not the absurdities of your management system. THEIR reality is real (your front line). Most of the answers you need are in the passion and intellectual capital of the people who work with you.

'What I'd suggest is that you try this ... Take three months and say to people, "Do what you think is right." It's about liberating your people to do what's right for the customer.

'Of course they will not always know the ramifications of what they want to do. This will force you to educate them in issues like profitability and the legal framework.

'You will find there are more opportunities to improve your business than to damage it by handing it over to the front line in this way. You will unlock a huge amount of customer insight. We did.

'If it fails the first time, understand why and do it again. You will need to adjust one or all of three things to get it to work:

1   the staff themselves;
2   the brief you give them; and
3   the environment in which they work.

This isn't a pipe dream. It worked for us ...'

*Inspired Leaders Network member
and Harley-Davidson Europe MD John Russell*

There are two concepts behind how Harley does business.

1   Act small

Large companies need to behave more like small companies. Leaders need to be more connected with their people and their customers than they currently are. Cynicism and functionalism, which you find in most large organizations, comes in reaction to the rules those companies breed.

2   Brands are built from the inside

... not from advertising campaigns. You can't expect to create a brand through advertising and the organization to fall in behind. The brand comes through in everything you do, including, say, your call answering system. 'Yes, we have one of those "Press button 2 for this and 3 for that" systems, but the very first thing you hear is, 'If you want to talk to a human being, press 1', says John Russell.

Out of these two concepts come some clear questions for leaders. First, what really is your customer proposition? John puts it this way: 'Life and work is stressful. Increasingly, people do not find work fulfilling enough. Our job is to offer freedom – an iconic, windswept and interesting spirit that is something very powerful in today's society. Our customer proposition isn't "a bike". We turn boring accountants into interesting people. Apologies to the accountants for the cheap shot …'

Then, how are you going to deliver on that proposition? Harley's starting point in answering this question is its customers. You have to revisit the company's roots to find the source of this enduring customer-centred approach. There were 200 motorbike companies in the US in the 1920s. There was one major-sized company left by the 1970s. The US bike industry's collapse, thanks to its inability to match Japanese quality and prices, has been well documented.

In the 1980s, the Harley turnaround began with a management buy-out. The company could hardly pay the wages when the Harley Owners Group (HOG) was born. It was the worst of times.

The company's new owners, its management, knew that its greatest asset was 300,000 customers. And that is where Harley was streets ahead of most other manufacturers. That's where its inspired leadership began. For most businesses, when times are tough, the last person they are thinking about is the customer. With Harley, the customer was where everything started from.

Ten lessons in how to lead a customer-centred organization come out of Harley's success from the 1980s onwards:

Ten leader's lessons *from Harley-Davidson*

1   Connect people's work to the vision

In 1983 the company's vision was 'We fulfil dreams'. Which means nothing without a business process. The company's leaders created one, which was cascaded down so that everyone's work assignments were connected to how they fulfilled the vision. Much of the success of the process – designing out quality problems, for example – was down to training the workforce in manufacturing methods like Statistical Process Control and then giving them the authority to control quality themselves. The first four days at Harley for every new recruit are spent learning the business process. Meetings always come back to the process.

2 Deal with the complexity

'KISS' (keep it simple, stupid) is true in execution. But it's not true when you're deciding what you need to do. Most organizations make decisions about what to do based on letting the interests of one stakeholder win at the expense of another (stockholders over customers, for example). But, at Harley, their tradition is to refuse to make decisions that way. They have to reach a solution that benefits all stakeholders. So it takes longer to reach solutions.

3 Research is no substitute for staying in touch

Research will never give you a deep enough context compared with being in your customers' shoes. All Harley executives are expected to ride with customers 10–15 days a year. At the 100th anniversary celebration in Milwaukee, the job of the company VPs was to hand out brochures for three days from a booth. One of the VPs told us that he worked out he had spoken to 10,000 customers, anonymously, over the three days. The authority of a job title is a handicap to bosses who want to get at the truth of what's going on.

4 Trade-offs are the essence of strong brands and culture

You have to make tough choices. Harley has 400 dealers in Europe, for example. It would be quick to grow through multi-franchise dealers. But, they wouldn't be able to offer the Harley-Davidson expertise and in-store experience. The company also pays its dealers more margin than the competition. The premium is a long term investment.

5 Let people behave like human beings

Corporations generally don't. It's only when there's a crisis that people pull together because their interests are suddenly aligned behind survival. Harley has a genuinely flat hierarchy. The most junior person can tell the CEO he's wrong and be listened to with respect. People are aligned behind the company's goal and allowed to be themselves.

6   Alignment and commitment

… come from strong values. Harley's five values have remained the same for over twenty years and are expressly designed to let people behave like human beings. They are:

- Tell the truth
- Be fair
- Keep promises
- Respect the individual
- Encourage curiosity.

7   Empowerment with accountability

… is possible. Most people will do the right thing if allowed to do so. You need rules, of course, such as Harley's rule that says, 'If you are going to make decisions, make sure you are competent in that area – get training if you feel you are not. And communicate with everyone else.'

8   Belonging drives customer and staff satisfaction

Knowing they are valued gives people self-confidence. Knowing they are trusted and share the values of the company gives a sense of belonging. Nothing builds satisfaction and loyalty like belonging.

9   Hierarchy inhibits customer understanding

Hierarchy must not be allowed to distort your understanding of the customer. Harley had a recall issue with Buell, a Harley brand, a few years ago. Most companies leave recalls to customer service and it's seen as an embarrassment. Harley issued six recall notices. John Russell says: 'One of our people came to us and said we should do more. Specifically, we should have a party for every customer who had had a problem with the recalled model. And we should do it at a race meeting. He would have been fired anywhere else. But, the hierarchy didn't get in the way. He was clearly right. He understood those customers. So, at every race meeting that season, we invited all Buell owners who had had a problem to join us for a party.'

10   Hierarchy inhibits employee contribution

Hierarchies act as a filter for the truth. Don't punish people for bad news. At Harley they say, 'Tell me true, tell me early'.

Harley's leaders insist that their success is down to a business process that allows people at the front line and on the assembly line to take the lead on behalf of customers, rather than down to the simple fact that the company's bikes have always been, er, way cool. And the facts back this up.

Yes, the company's bikes have been icons of cool since at least Dennis Hopper and Peter Fonda brought them to mainstream attention in *Easy Rider*, and probably long before that. But, it was only after the company set up customer-centred business processes and gave control to people on the front line that its profits started to take off.

And John Russell is right: no matter how boring your industry, you can inject a sense of 'wow' and buzz into it by taking the lead in re-designing your customer experience around a distinctive proposition. It can be as boring as nails or paint or PC maintenance. It's the theatre you construct around it that creates the compelling story that attracts customers to you. We're not talking PR here. We're not talking advertising. We're talking a themed customer experience.

It is in breaking with Taylorism and principles of scientific management that inspired leaders create and lead customer-aligned organizations like Virgin and Harley-Davidson. In that sense, inspired leaders are post-industrial.

Sense and respond

Where do you start? Try your call centre. It's where your customers are likely to be experiencing the most pain. Contact centres have traditionally been run on the same scientific management principles as late 19th century factories, with calls treated as the unit of production. And we all know how successful that has been. Jamie Lywood, one of our members, runs a company that records call centre experiences, analyzes them to give them a customer empathy rating, then plays them back to the board. Jamie calls himself a customer empathy architect. It's the new frontier.

Call centres, along with a surprisingly large number of other desk-based jobs, are actually conceived on factory principles. Even in banking, for example, products are developed, then thrown over the wall to the operations people who have to deliver them, and to the marketing people who communicate them to the customer. It's *push*, based on the company's perceived need, not *pull* based on the customer's.

Just as manufacturers have had to move away from the Fordist principles underlying mass production, you have to do the same to match the needs of 21st century employees, customers and partners. You have to change the system that is rooted in productionist principles of the 20th century, so that employees can sense and respond to changes in the market they are dealing with, one customer at a time. *How the work works* needs to change.

Toyota pioneered the use of 'pull' principles by letting the demand side of the market pull through components and products instead of planning and pushing through what you think will be needed by customers. And hence, lean production was born. The litany of lean production became familiar in the west through the late 1980s and 1990s as the US and Northern Europe frantically tried to learn what Japan had originally learnt from a maverick American who couldn't make himself heard above the Fordist din in his home country.[9]

Systems thinking

The challenge for leaders looking to shape their organizations to deliver a customer experience is to use systems thinking, to re-design how your work flows and who controls it. The objective is to enable work to be pulled through by customer demand. This has to be within set parameters and with the right customers, of course, otherwise you can be pulled out of shape by responding to inappropriate demands.[10]

From First Direct Bank to Fujitsu, an increasing number of our members have turned to systems thinking as a powerful tool for 21st century leaders wanting to break free from the more limiting productionist thinking of last century. At the core of systems thinking is the principle 'Act on the system, not the individual'.

So, for example, incentive programmes based on hitting targets assume that you need to change individual behaviour to improve performance. But, if those individuals have to deliver those targets within an unchanged system, and they are ambitious targets that your system failed to hit before, you are often simply setting your people up to fail. Or, since most people want to avoid failure, you distort their behaviour. They cheat or focus on hitting the targets at the expense of other value generation that may be more important.

Two examples:

1   The National Health Service in the UK has used targets to try to reduce the length of time patients have to wait for treatment. The effect in many cases was a distortion of what was happening on the ground, just to hit the targets. In some cases, the figures were actually massaged. Strange new practices emerged, such as patients waiting to be put on the waiting list(!), so that the local hospital would hit its waiting list targets.[11]

2   Senior executives and CEOs commonly set ambitious targets, then distort business activity by focusing on actions designed to deliver spectacular short-term figures, in order to hit those targets, at the expense of longer term value creation. Merger and acquisition activity is the obvious example. You end up playing the numbers game instead of leading.[12]

Assembly line of the mind

So, you constantly need to beware the assembly line of the mind. Quality monitoring, targets and many of your other management tools can lead you to slipping into playing the numbers game, losing sight of the actual value of what your people do and how to motivate them. The biggest challenge is to break away from this list of typical ways of thinking (below). Recognize any of them?

Examples of systemic 'wrongthink'

- This change is too big or difficult.
- You need to be at the top of the organization to influence large-scale change.
- You are doing OK because your internal measures are fine.
- Your people are too dumb to help create a better system.
- Your people don't cheat in order to survive the current system.
- Empowerment is something you give.
- Transformation is all very well in a text book but it cannot happen in real life.
- You are customer-focused.
- Individuals have control over their own performance.
- Mass-production thinking.

The inspired leader gets around this list of obstacles by navigating using the principle of external customer control, instead of internal hierarchical control. In other words, acknowledge when re-designing your system that the customer needs to be in control, which means decision-making moves down to the front line, away from management. Because, the front line is where the customers are, with your front line people doing business for you one customer at a time. It's hard for many managers to acknowledge that their role is not to accumulate power anymore, but to support front line people in exercising their own decision-making.

Front line leadership

In fact, the closer leaders are to the front line, the more effective they tend to be. Yet, in most organizations, seniority is denoted by distance *from* the front line. Dealing with customers is for junior people. If that's your prevailing culture, then you're in trouble. Jan Carlzon, author of the seminal book *Moments of Truth*, recounted how he began the turnaround of the then-troubled SAS (Scandinavian Airline System) by acting in a way that his fellow board members initially thought was eccentric to say the least.

Carlzon spent a couple of weeks simply mingling with customers, joining them in line in airport terminals, sitting next to them anonymously on flights. 'I just looked for where our customers were and hung around with them', he said. Everywhere he went, Carlzon took a notepad and pen. And he jotted down his own experiences, those he observed other customers going through, and the conversations he overheard. This was the beginning of the notion of mapping the customer experience and identifying the so-called 'touch points' with your organization that determine how the customer feels about their overall experience.[13] What was significant about Carlzon's actions was that it wasn't a market researcher out there doing the mapping on the ground. It was the CEO.

Ford COO Sir Nick Scheele echoes this idea that leaders have to put themselves on the front line if they are to truly understand what is going on in their business. Here's what he told us:

Feel your customer's pain

'When I was in charge of Jaguar, I used to use the trip home to listen to tapes we had made of customers calling in with a complaint. I remember driving home and cringing as I listened to one particular call.

It was a woman describing how she had to climb out of the sun roof of her car, in the pouring rain, slide down the windscreen and off the bonnet, because the electronic door locks of her Jaguar had seized up, trapping her in.

You can imagine the state of mind she was in; the distress that our product had created.

'Leaders belong on the front line'

And it was only through hearing directly from the customer that I partially shared that state of mind, was allowed into it.

It is common practice for senior managers to be shielded from customers, for middle managers to be intermediaries processing customer satisfaction ratings and market research findings and presenting them to the Boss in a neatly bound report.

If that is how you work, then you are not in touch with your customers, and therefore not in touch with the reality of your business. You have to hear direct from customers to realize where the critical path lies for improvements to your business.

If you have intermediaries between you and your customers, your market, then you are too far removed from their pain to take swift action.'

Ford COO and President Sir Nick Scheele

It's not just the CEO or top tier who need to be exposed to customer pain like this. The principle Scheele recommends for encouraging leadership at all levels is to remove the anonymity associated with assembly line practices. Link actions with consequences by handing responsibility to individuals who do the actual work.

One of the changes Scheele helped to introduce at Jaguar, for example, was that if a customer had a complaint or comment about how a particular part of the car worked – the door handle or driver's seat or window opener – they would receive a call back from the person working in the actual factory who had installed that particular part of the car, so that person could learn from the customer experience and make improvements.

The most successful leaders today shape an organization that has, as the CEO of Europe's Carphone Warehouse, Charles Dunstone, describes it, 'a customer in every decision'. Dunstone points to the obvious problem that when you are big, it's too easy to become distant from the people who deliver the service. So, part of a senior manager's role is to use their weight to exert downward pressure on the hierarchy by adopting a default position that sides with the front line. 'My role is to side with the people in the stores against everyone else in the organization,' says Dunstone candidly.

You're not a supplier

Much of this book is about the dismantling of borders. Or at least recognizing those borders are no longer there and leading accordingly. The imaginary line that runs around an organization, with customers on the outside, is one such border. The boundary of a company (if we ignore a legalistic definition for our purposes here) is based on notions of a supplier/customer divide, with transactions taking place across that divide. Life's not that simple anymore.

It comes back again to the distinction that last century was a (supplier) push economy and this century is largely a (customer) pull economy. With this shift in dynamics, the very word 'supplier' starts to blur around the edges. The phrase 'demand chain' began to appear in the 1990s in recognition of this shift in power. Inspired leaders go one step further than anyone else and take this to its logical conclusion.

The UK supermarket giant Tesco[14] now describes itself not as a supplier, but as *a buyer on behalf of its customers*. This isn't just some kind of wordplay for the sake of it. In a pull economy the flow of power and control is reversed. Most organizations, however, still operate as if power flows from the supply-side. You either go with the flow by turning around and re-defining yourself out of the supplier space, or you inadvertently create an organization that is constantly clashing with customers – a customer adversarial organization – because you haven't recognized the current has reversed.

You are what you eat

Under CEO Sir Terry Leahy,[15] you can even argue that Tesco is now a medium, not a store, one of the few remaining unfragmented media at that. Customer buying patterns flow up from the (super)market to Tesco's suppliers. Instead of finding customers for its products, Tesco has become the medium that translates customer needs back to those suppliers to develop the next set of products for customers, for which it then acts as the access and delivery channel.

The retailer achieves this neat re-invention trick through consensual data collection, which is analyzed and fed back to Tesco's suppliers, telling them whether their product is going to be a success or not. The company touches its customers ten million times a week in its stores. It runs a whole series of customized direct mail programmes. It knows 40% of its customers' email addresses. 'Tesco don't want to go off and develop thousands of new products. They'd much rather their suppliers did that', observes Clive

Humby, who helped develop the Tesco Clubcard strategy that delivers all this data.

Jean Brillan-Savarin, the French gastronome, wrote *The Physiology of Taste* in 1801. In it he coined the expression, 'You are what you eat'. What he actually said was 'Tell me what you eat and I will tell you what you are'. And that, says Clive Humby, is the essence of how Tesco gets intimate with its customers. 'You know how you can't resist looking at the contents of the basket in front of you when you are in a checkout line in a supermarket. And you make sub-conscious assumptions about the lives of the people who are buying that stuff. Well, that's what I spend all my working time doing, essentially', says Clive. 'We find patterns in the data that our customers consensually supply to us.'

A life more ordinary

Something else is going on 'out there' that's odd and needs you to turn some of your assumptions on their head. It's the rise of the Everyman millionaire; the customers who insist you treat them as celebrities. In the US, entrepreneur Debbi Fields built up a multi-million dollar chain of retail cookie outlets. She trains her people to imagine the actress Julia Roberts is walking into their store every time a customer comes in. 'Have you seen how people's faces light up in the presence of celebrity and how the normal rules no longer apply? People do what's required to please them', she says. Who wants to be a millionaire? Everyone, apparently.

This is not as superficial as it sounds. Celebrity (when it's not about sexual attraction) is about projecting our own need for recognition in a crowded world onto someone else. Living vicariously and all that. Customers are increasingly demanding, discerning, intolerant and want your customer proposition shaped to their needs – just like celebrities. Fields' observation runs deeper than it first appears. There is, in fact, an economic sea change going on here. You can sum it up as the collapse of the Richness versus Reach equation.

Tesco and Wal-Mart are the perfect retail examples of high quality at low price. Sam Walton, in fact, famously defined Wal-Mart's purpose as being to allow poorer people to buy the same things and live the same kinds of lives as only the rich had been allowed to participate in before Wal-Mart came along. Essentially, we're back to commoditization again. Only, now we're anticipating the tipping point at which, say, giant flat-screen plasma TVs migrate from being millionaire rock star toys to commodities adorning the walls of every room in everybody's house in the developed world (which they inevitably will; by the time you are reading this, maybe they already have).

Mass wealth?

Financial services companies are struggling with the democratization of wealth management. The Customer Relationship Management models that emerged towards the end of the last century assumed that segmentation would be based on a richer experience for more valued customers (personal banking, up to a point) and a low-cost, shallower customer experience (Interactive Voice Response, for example) for the 80% or more that are perceived as low value.

But, this model has struggled to take off. It has partly been warped by the new trade-off between Richness and Reach that customers are getting a taste of through digital-based services. And, it is partly failing because all bank customers want the luxury of personal service and being treated as special. They just don't want to pay for it. Everyone wants personal banking and they want it for free. Egg, the financial services organization designed for the digital economy, defines Richness and Reach this way:

- *Richness* in Financial Services = More Personal, More Choice, More Service
- *Reach* in Financial Services = Keener Pricing, More Simplicity

Traditional sources of profit in financial services – products and distribution networks – are put at risk by the fact that the cost advantages of the digital economy allow eFinancial Services players to deliver both. Egg's former Chief Marketing Officer, one of our members, gives us this example of the resulting category collapse: 'There were two kinds of savings account – Instant Access or Notice. With the former, the customer had to sacrifice interest for access. For the latter, the customer had to sacrifice access for interest. So, we launched a near-instant access account with notice-level interest to break this category distinction. It brought us 600,000 customers in six months'.[16]

Find the moment

Inspired leaders go further still, pioneering a new form of permission marketing. Don Peppers has a calculation that shows how marketing campaigns, even those informed by CRM systems that customize the offer a little, based on some knowledge of the customer, can erode customer value in ways that simply aren't measured. A two-month direct mail campaign may net, say, $50,000 above and beyond the cost of the campaign. But, say the campaign had a 2% response rate. What this form of marketing fails to measure is the decline in propensity to buy from you among the 98% who didn't respond, a significant proportion of whom have been alienated from you, even by a degree or so, because of your unsolicited approach. And, in many cases, that erosion of customer value will outstrip the profit you made from the campaign.

So, inspired leaders practise a different form of customer engagement. They let the customer decide the timing of offers to them. Kari Opdal, in charge of customer management at Union Bank of Norway, says you need to stop bombarding existing and potential customers with traditional marketing and evolve to the next level, in which the customer initiates the dialogue.

Kari's bank has one million customers, a quarter of the population of Norway. She asked herself this question: 'Why are all bank communications bank-driven; going out as part of a campaign to hit targets like "move 100,000 credit cards in July?" We were guilty: planning campaigns at the beginning of the year. "In March, we'll push mortgages. Over the summer, we'll push credit cards as it's holiday time." But, now we've changed. We have shifted to running campaigns year-round, but finding the moment for each customer when it is right. We have one million segments of one.'

Complicity rules

Kari's customers agreed to fill in a major questionnaire about themselves once, and then update it annually in return for special treatment such as preferential interest rates. And they agreed to be contacted if their questionnaire and/or account movements indicated a significant life event, such as a redundancy payment, pay bonus, house move, child being born or an older child heading off to university. Kari's IT systems run overnight, analyzing account movements among her customers that day and sending out relevant suggestions to banking staff to follow up next morning, based on the data for individual customers.

So, this new-style marketing isn't based on products. It's based on contact triggered by individual customer life-events, with the customer's permission in advance and some kind of explicit customer benefit (reduced interest rates in this case). It's the opt-in world taken to the next level. Conversion rates are a staggering 40%, as opposed to typical direct mail results of less than 2%. The divorce rate in Norway's capital, Oslo, is 50%. Kari's people are trying to work out non-intrusive ways of approaching customers at this stage of their relationship to help them sort out their finances as one customer becomes two. They haven't worked out how to do it tactfully yet.

Significantly, Kari says she was given the freedom to create this new approach by her CEO, whose brief to her was simply, 'Go make footprints'. Other banks weren't getting it right. So, Kari was given the freedom to invent a new way of letting customers take the lead.

CRM is just wallpaper

OK, we've mentioned CRM systems twice in this chapter so far without being rude about them. But, we just can't hold ourselves back any longer. 'CRM is just wallpaper. Thinking that IT-driven CRM can help your customer relationship problems is like thinking re-decorating can save your marriage,' says Clive Humby.

It's not just that so many IT systems that claim to be about CRM started off as something else – Sales Force Automation (SFA) systems many of them were called until the leaders of major corporations began looking for customer solutions they could buy off the shelf – though that has a lot to do with it.

In 2003, Phil Walker, a partner at IBM Global Business Services, was among a gathering of 5,000 IBM-ers, each of whom had the word 'customer' somewhere in their job title. He came to speak to us afterwards. They had, he said, come together to thrash out what comes after CRM. 'There is a new customer space and it's about three things', said Phil:

1   *Spock was wrong*. Feelings matter. We have to acknowledge that emotions play a part in decisions, even in business.
2   *Listening shows you care*. Historically, supplying wasn't about listening. Particularly in Northern Europe and the USA, where hitherto our role as exporters gives us a traditional supplier mentality we need to break from.
3   *Realism*. Technology alone won't engender a relationship. At IBM we have to stop having meetings where we decide whether to sell someone Siebel or something else from our portfolio and take the discussion wider.

The rational blue-suits are having to learn another language. It's human CRM if you like. And it still won't deliver loyalty. If you want loyalty, get a dog. We're in the age of what Regis McKenna called 'the never-satisfied customer'.[17] Even putting aside arguments about whether satisfaction delivers loyalty (it doesn't[18]), the question you have to constantly answer from your customers, no matter how much they like you at the moment, was best-framed by Janet Jackson: 'What have you done for me lately?'

CRM for free

To end this chapter, here's a leader's secret that'll help you save millions by delivering CRM for free! What's more, it involves no IT and the idea didn't even come from the top ...

CRM is a state of mind

Years ago, when Ritz-Carlton was one of the only hotel chains with a working customer recognition system, Roger Dow, the Senior Marketing VP at Marriott, asked the IT people how much it would cost to recognize returning customers so they could be greeted personally, prompted by the check-in screen. '$2 million and it'll take two years' was the reply. 'You're joking!' stormed Dow and headed off on an unannounced tour of Marriotts.

At one provincial hotel the bellboy welcomed him at his car and took his bag through to reception. Dow reached the desk a few seconds later. 'Welcome back, sir. It's good to have you with us again,' said the desk clerk. 'What!' said Dow. 'Do you know who I am?' 'No, sir,' replied the clerk, thinking she had done something wrong.'How on earth did you know I've been here before? I'm the senior VP in charge of marketing and I've been trying to get the IT people to allow us to welcome people back and it's too expensive!' bellowed Dow.

'Well, we have our own system here, sir,' said the clerk. 'When the bellboy welcomes you at your car he asks if it is your first time here. You must have said that you'd been here before. When he drops the bag here at the desk, he winks at me if you're a returning visitor. Then I know to welcome you back …'.[19]

This chapter drew on the thinking and practice of the following Inspired Leaders Network members and friends:

John Russell
European MD, Harley-Davidson.

Don Peppers
Partner, Peppers & Rogers.

Kate Stanners
Creative Director, St. Luke's Advertising Agency.

Professor Merlin Stone
IBM & Bristol Business School.

Nick Potts
IBM. Nick was formerly HR Director at Virgin Atlantic.

Jamie Lywood
Group CEO, Harding & Yorke plc.

Lyell Strambi
COO, Virgin Atlantic.

Steve Parry
Head of Strategy, Fujitsu Europe.

Sir Nick Scheele
COO & President, Ford.

Kari Opdal
Head of CRM, Union Bank of Norway.

Charles Dunstone
CEO, Carphone Warehouse.

Clive Humby
Chairman, Dunnhumby, a company now owned by Tesco. Clive explains how Tesco developed its data-driven approach in his book *Scoring Points: How Tesco is winning customer loyalty.*

Richard Duvall
Former CMO, Egg. Richard is profiled in Patricia Seybold's book *The Customer Revolution* as a creator of revolutionary business forms.

Phil Walker
Till recently Partner, IBM Global Business Services. Now a VP at Cap Gemini.

There's nothing out there

This chapter in 30 seconds

Disney was right. It's a small world, after all. This chapter offers insights into how to lead your organization in a shrinking world, where the borders that need dismantling are mostly borders of the mind. Just as importantly, it will explain why you can't buy Heinz ketchup in Poland.

Still see global business in terms of geographic boundaries, multi-nationals, import/export, a home territory and the regions? That's s-o-o-o last century. Inspired leaders see the world differently. There's a new global soup out there. Come on in; the water's lovely.

Should your strategy in this brave (read 'scary') new world be global, local or glocal? Probably all three. Or maybe HSBC's multi-local is the way to go.

20th century business globalism was largely Americanism, expansionism, McGlobalism. The struggle is on to see if this will be the next American Century. Choose carefully where you stand.

There's nothing out there

On ... the return of the middle kingdom, the death of geography, glocalism and beyond, Old Europe, a world of contrasts, the new foreign legion, why Small is the new Big, Amex's 3-Tier Globalism, Shell's 100 Year Delta, a 30-second inspired history of global brands, and how to be everywhere at once.

Time for a whistle-stop global tour of the new world of business: 'It's 4pm, we must be in Helsinki', that kind of thing. So, you have to promise not to blink as you read, because there's a lot of ground to cover in a few pages and you might miss a global trend or two that will jump up and bite you later.

Let's start with something weird: the maps are re-drawing themselves. If you have a world map on your office wall somewhere (shame on you if you haven't), have you noticed the countries moving? There's a kind of accelerated plate tectonics going on. They are scooting around that map like Michael Schumacher when your back is turned. What was at the centre of your world? Take another look and you'll find it's been displaced.

The return of the middle kingdom

'China is the middle kingdom at the centre of the map on my wall', says Andrew Fraser, senior adviser to Mitsubishi. Andrew used to be in charge of inward investment to the UK. From his new perspective, Manhattan is the Far East. Only it's not a new perspective. It's an old one that has come around full circle again. In the 17th century China was the world's largest economy. It will be again.

The gravitational pull of China's fast-growing economy is exerting previously unforeseen effects as we write – sucking up raw materials in vast amounts, even forcing up the global price of steel. Forcing UP the price of steel? Who'd have thought it? The relentless downward price-pull of commoditization, one of the most reliable forces in global economics, has been suspended and temporarily reversed by the power of China's growth engine.

Andrew says you need to look for similar examples of a suspension of the way global business works, or used to work, to break yourself out of outmoded notions that shackle you and limit your room for manoeuvre.

We have moved on a long way from when Ted Levitt first described globalism as selling the same things to everyone everywhere. What Goldman Sachs calls the Brics – Brazil, Russia, India, China – made not a dent in the rest of the world's business consciousness not so long ago. Yet China and India, in particular, have moved from the edge to the centre of the map. There's been a marked acceleration in the speed of this global change. That's what we mean by the maps re-drawing themselves.

Manufacturing is everywhere

If Big Change Number One is in how you look at the map, the second change in the way global business works is that there is no advantage in manufacturing anymore. Anything can be made anywhere. Well, almost. Importing raw materials from countries that lack their own production facilities, making things and exporting finished products back to them is a busted flush. It's not just last century, it's the one before that.

Quality is everywhere too, thanks to everyone copying Japan, as well as that country exporting its own techniques by establishing plants outside Japan's borders. Back in the 1970s it took Sony a decade to bring its Welsh manufacturing plant up to the quality levels of its home plants. It took the same company just six months from moving into manufacturing in Poland and Slovakia to bring those countries' operations up to the required level. The knock-on effect up the supply chain in these countries is now well documented. Indeed, one of our members, the head of Unipart's

Corporate University, Frank Nigriello, explained to our Network recently how Unipart, which used to supply parts exclusively to the UK carmaker Rover, staked the business on becoming accepted as a supplier to two Japanese carmakers.

The point was not to make a profit, as these were demanding customers. It was survival: 'They wouldn't tell us how to "do" quality – we asked if we could visit and learn from them and they refused. So we focused everything on becoming suppliers to these companies to force quality into our company that way, as we knew they educated and trained their supply chain in their practices', he explained.

Therefore, if you are or were in manufacturing, your globalism strategy has to be robust enough to take on:

- Overcapacity
- Commoditization
- The consequent drive for differentiation
- The need to compete on services and intangibles.

According to Tom Peters, Sara Lee, manufacturer of everything from frozen cakes to Kiwi shoe polish, has said it is getting out of making things and will become a virtually asset-less company, as there is no competitive advantage in manufacturing.

Geography is dead

Business is borderless. Of course, there are still barriers to the free movement of goods, but look behind the movement of goods and services. It's the movement of investment across the world that has demolished borders. Corporates who were fundamentally committed to their home market now find themselves stateless.

About 8% of Nokia is in Finnish ownership. Its heart, soul and driving force may be within Finland. But its owners are not. Assets are now truly global. Foreign assets made up 60% of the world's GDP in 1995. Andrew Fraser's research suggests it's up another 15% or so since then. Everywhere we find the pull of borderless investment breaking down barriers of the mind linked to country borders.

We've seen this for decades in behind-the-scenes movements of vast amounts of capital, such as GM taking controlling stakes in nation-based carmakers like Saab, Vauxhall and Australia's Holden. The practice through the latter decades of the 20th century, as the American car giants faced limited growth opportunities at home, was to trophy-hunt for foreign marques. General Motors and Ford would buy up carmakers abroad that were national symbols to their consumers, keep the badge and the national brand values, while taking advantage of global sourcing to use common platforms and car parts across a range of badges.

It's not just the Americans doing the buying. Old Europe turned the tables with Daimler's takeover of Chrysler. No, it wasn't a merger, by the way. That myth lasted a couple of weeks before the mask slipped and it became clear this was Old Europe moving, unwelcome, into a section of America's industrial homeland. As the joke doing the rounds of Ford's HQ in Dearborn, Michigan, at the time put it:

> **'How do you pronounce DaimlerChrysler?**
> **The "Chrysler" is silent.'**

The difference in recent years is that the sleight of hand is less convincing. We're back to the transparency issue. When Ford bought the UK luxury car marque Jaguar, it had to defend itself against loyal Jaguar customers who banded together and demanded assurance that their prized marque would not end up as a Jaguar skin hiding parts shared with Ford models such as the Mondeo and Focus. Modern consumers know far more about what is going on and are challenging supplier-driven models in which pricing and sales structures vary from country to country.

British car buyers started to notice in the 1990s that cars are several thousand pounds cheaper in mainland Europe (for complex reasons, partly due to the over-developed company car fleet market in the UK). So, they challenged the structure, exerting downward pressure on UK prices by starting to import their own cars, one customer at a time. Consumers are practising their own form of global sourcing, subverting big company national sales structures in the process.

In parts of central London it's not possible to buy a can of Coke with English writing on it. Slovenian, yes. Arabic, yes. English, no. This isn't sophisticated targeting for London's Slovenian-reading population. It's retailers by-passing Coke's official distribution channels and buying their stock from grey importers who make a profit from Coke's differential pricing. When Coke launched Vanilla Coke into the UK market with a megabucks advertising and marketing campaign, it wasn't that big a surprise to consumers, who had been buying grey import bottles of the stuff for months.

The nation firm is homeless

Consumers are being weaned away from the security of a world viewed through the playpen bars of reassuring national boundaries to the less secure notion that we can, in some senses, be everywhere at once. It's a connected world. Charles Schwab ran adverts in Australia pointing up the need to invest beyond the domestic market, saying 'You can't win with investments concentrated in just 1% of the global capital market.'

The important thing, said Robert Reich, Clinton's Labour Secretary, is not which nations own what, but which nations know how to do what. The nation firm is now homeless. The mental model of the world that most managers use when they think of how to lead their organization internationally is one of exports and imports – whether that be of goods, services, jobs or people. But this mental model is increasingly inadequate to deal with the opportunities and threats that *worldshrink* brings to your front door. As Peter Drucker pointed out recently, the model of the multinational firm, based in one country with outposts in others, largely unchanged since the early 20th century, is of decreasing relevance.[1]

Despite all the talk of a borderless world, despite the assertions of luminaries such as Anita Roddick that business can do more to change how the world works than governments, don't accept the rhetoric about the state being increasingly irrelevant. Some of our members predict a possible return of Big Government, particularly when it comes to state interference in cross-border business. By the oxymoron 'possible prediction' we mean, of course, that we

are in a place-your-bets situation. When the world is less predictable, you need to anticipate a range of alternative possible futures,
or at least be able to identify and better understand some of the
forces that may affect your business.

Shell pioneered *scenario planning* in the 1970s as a tool for navigating an increasingly uncertain future, of course. Each scenario is
a powerful global *zeitgeist* or context within which you may have
to do business, rather than a prediction of how the world will be. If
you already practise scenarios or something similar, then skip the
next couple of paragraphs, as we don't want to teach you how to
suck eggs.

Avoid futureshock

With scenario planning, an unlikely global trend may indeed
emerge and knock your business sideways. You can then survey
the wreckage and say knowingly, 'Ah, yes, we were scuppered.
But, at least we had anticipated that we might be, with scenario
number 84.'

Seriously though … scenario planning has its uses when the
global soup churns so fast you can't figure out where the next
wave of change will come from or what shape it will be. Mary Jo
Jacobi is a former trade adviser to two US Presidents – Reagan and
Bush the elder. Mary Jo is now with Shell and outlined to us two of
Shell's scenarios for the 'noughties' (the first ten years of this century) and beyond, one of which includes a reassertion of national
governments' influence over cross-border business.

It is called the Prism scenario. 'In this scenario', explains Mary
Jo, 'economic liberalization in and of itself, isn't trusted. Governments re-emerge as a more powerful force than they have been
in recent times. And these governments are expected to nurture
social cohesion while still delivering economic progress. Countries
find their own development paths. As a consequence, environments for businesses vary from country to country, similar to the
environment that we operate in today.'

The 'Prism' scenario describes a world that's shaped not by what
we have in common but by the interplay of our differences. In it,
people react to globalization by emphasizing their cultural roots.

They are still interested in economic well-being, and in growth, but wary of being Americanized, it seems.

Pick your own future

A second world scenario Shell came up with for the near-future is 'Business Class', which describes a world that's focused on efficiency and individual freedom of choice. It's shaped by a highly interconnected and ever-expanding global elite and is largely influenced by US values, ideas and ethics. In a Business Class future, companies are global and globalization is seen to provide widespread benefits. Regulation focuses on market efficiency. Increasing inequality is tolerated as long as people see opportunities to improve their lot – a very American perspective.

They've got lots of other scenarios if you don't like those two. That's the beauty of scenario planning for the global economy. It's a bit like conflicting scientific opinion. You can pick the one you like best. Just make sure you've got yourself covered if it turns out to be the wrong one. Whether you use scenario planning or other tools for reducing the impact of global uncertainty, inspired leaders keep their organization flexible enough to ride the waves of change that the unpredictable global economy throws at them, rather than believing they can define and impose a rigid globalist strategy. You simply don't have that level of control anymore. Here's more on how it works at Shell.

Shell's 100 year delta

Despite the rhetoric about fast companies and agility being a 21st century attribute, Shell still has to plan 20 years ahead. The timescales from first exploration to the first drops of oil coming out of the ground to the depletion of the source and the last drops being pumped are measured in decades, if not a century. In Nigeria, for example, Shell is around halfway through its anticipated 100-year time horizon of involvement with the country.

Hence the value Shell places on scenario planning.

Three forces

The scenarios aren't mutually exclusive predictions – that the world will look like either Business Class or Prism. They are descriptions of likely emerging currents that the company needs to be ready to ride if necessary in order to continue to thrive in these environments. The currents are driven largely by three forces:

- Globalization
- Liberalization
- Technology

Nowhere to hide

Of these three forces, globalism leaves you nowhere to hide. Recent polls have shown that large companies are less trusted than politicians. Shell learned in 1995 that instant global availability of information means if your reputation is damaged somewhere it is damaged everywhere. That was the year in which environmental activists from Greenpeace boarded the Brent Spar, a floating oil storage structure Shell was about to dump at sea. Under a global media spotlight, Shell negotiated an alternative (and far more expensive) de-commissioning plan for the rig.

Local reputation management

… is global reputation management. As a result of the Brent Spar crisis, managing Shell's reputation in-country was made a prime responsibility of country managers, rather than a corporate PR issue. To avoid a local issue spiralling out of control, a global company has to be close to local concerns, runs the logic. Reputation management is increasingly seen by leading corporates as part of risk management, not PR.

Trust me, I'm in oil

The oil giant tracks what its retail customers feel is Shell's most important brand attribute. It used to be simply 'that the station is located at a convenient point'. Now that has given way to 'Can I trust your brand?'

Global buy-in

All of Shell's employees around the world sign up to the company's values once a year – literally. They all sign to say they have read and complied with the company's statement of business principles; how it does business around the globe (including 'no bribes', even if it's local custom and practice ...).

And yet, and yet ...
Cleaning up your global act in a business like oil doesn't happen overnight. Shell still attracts protests at its shareholder meetings in Europe as a result of its close relations with the former military government of Nigeria that executed activist Ken Saro-Wiwa in 1995. Saro-Wiwa had championed the grievances of the indigenous Ogoni people in the Niger delta, where much of Shell's oil production is concentrated. And signing up to the company's values didn't stop Shell's chairman, Sir Philip Watts, overstating Shell's oil reserves and having to resign in 2004 as a result.

More Shell scenarios on the web
http://www.shell.com

Now, let's switch horses and see how Jesse James can help us make sense of the world.

Jesse James's mission statement

'I rob banks because that's where the money is.'

Jesse James

Jesse James's mission statement was nothing if not focused. So, where will the money be for businesses as the 21st century progresses? If 'show me the money' in a global context means 'show me the educated and affordable warm bodies', India's population, to take one figure here, is growing more in a week than the European Union's does in a year. India already produces 10% of the world's drugs and dominates the generic pharmaceuticals market. The world's pharma companies moved production to India because it was cheap. Now they're moving their new R&D labs there because the research scientists are as good as or better than anywhere in the world (and because they are still cheap).

India produces three million IT graduates annually, more than half the working population of Sweden.[2]

So, if the 20th century was dubbed 'The American Century' in recognition of the US as the dominant economic, will the 21st century develop into 'The Indian Century'? One thing looks more certain at the moment; if population age equates with economic vitality, it won't be 'The European Century' without some radical action. US Secretary of State Donald Rumsfeld famously dismissed France and Germany as 'Old Europe'. It turns out he was right. In demographic terms, anyway. If you're focused on doing business in Europe, learn how to sell to pensioners. Penniless pensioners at that.

Germany is the extreme example:

- 21.7% of the population were over 65 in 1999
- 49.2% will be over 65 by 2030

Yet that country's pension assets as a proportion of its GDP are pretty negligible. It looks as if two Germans will be left working and supporting the rest of the population in a few decades. Which, of course, feeds into the current debate on 'export jobs or import people'. Suddenly immigration doesn't look so threatening after all, if the social security contributions of these new workers will be paying the pensions of the ageing indigenous community who so often argue for keeping the newcomers out.

Would that it were that simple to break down this particular border of the mind. There is a growing trend within economics that we find interesting: an admission that the *hard* side of economics has been overstated, and the *soft side* – the psychology that drives people behaviour at an individual and at a macro level – virtually discounted, precisely because it can't be counted. Economics assumes we behave *en masse* as rational beings. We don't, of course.

Import people or export jobs

The offshoring debate – the global redistribution of work and value generation that has moved up the business and political agenda in recent years – is at the heart of the new debate on what constitutes globalism. One of the choices facing government and business leaders is the 'export jobs or import people' question. But, the very framing of this question betrays a one-sided perspective. Offshoring is a statist word. It frames itself with the borders of the state as the reference point.[3]

The interesting thing is not so much corporations lowering their costs by sending jobs to where people are cheaper – there is nothing new in that; it has just moved up the chain from making clothes to taking calls to writing code and designing drugs. What's as interesting, but less commented on, is the growth of a new generation of global citizens who have the skills and outlook to go wherever they want. You are probably one of this global elite, so this aspect of globalization is directly relevant to you.

Kjell Nordström, the Swedish economist, was presenting to one of our corporate clients recently, giving them a private lecture on how to cope with the new globalism. So, we collared him in the break and asked him for some enlightenment on what he calls 'the foreign legion' syndrome. Nordström neatly re-frames the debate away from the narrow 'all our jobs are going abroad' kneejerk reaction by focusing on geographical clustering (see Michael Porter's recent work for more on clustering).

'You can find the place you fit in the world now', said Nordström. 'For example, 73% of people working in Silicon Valley weren't born in the US. They moved there. They are a foreign legion. This is globalism in action. It's self-selection. There are thousands of valleys around the world – the financial valley of Wall Street or London, the fashion valley concentrated in Emilio Romagna, Northern Italy.

'People think globalization is global corporations rolling out a global brand – McDonald's, Marlboro – that's not just wrong, it's exactly wrong. Globalism is about more fragmented, different markets; you have to go back to medieval city states to find markets as fragmented. The question in the face of such fragmentation is: Can you run a company based on principles of standardization and global brands, or do you need to take a different route?'[4]

Pause to stargaze

Back to our global tour. But before we look at an example of South African globalism, we'd like to stop and look upwards to help us on the whole issue of global perspective. The idea of the world being 'out there' to be toured and your business having to go out to sell to it is at the heart of the weakness in global business thinking. Increasingly, the world is on your doorstep, or in your own backyard, or sitting down next to you, whichever metaphor helps you frame the issues more effectively. It's like those horror movies where the occupants of a house spend all their time peering out of through locked windows and doors, waiting for a slasher *out there* to come and get them, whereas we, the viewers, know he's actually already in the attic. Since much global thinking is still framed in terms of *self* and *other,* with the rest of the world inevitably being cast as the other, the explicit threat in the house of horror metaphor is pertinent. The reality is that 'there is no there, there', as Gertrude Stein once remarked about the American Midwest. Global is local.

To reinforce this death-of-geography point, it may help to borrow a perspective from physics. To do so helps you to hold this strange notion in your head: that you can be, in a business sense, everywhere at the same time, without moving from where you are. The weird science that helps you frame this perspective is stargazing.

If it's a useful image that inspires you to think differently about globalism, then retain it. If not, move swiftly on. Here goes: Stare at a star. It is untold millions of miles away, right? It's light years away. The distance is inconceivable. Yet, matter from that star, converted into light waves, is hitting the back of your eye and being absorbed into your body. Cosmic, man … Global business today is like that. It's not out there. You're inside it and it's inside you.

All the corporates have the technology to make everyone everywhere part of a globally distributed head office, using intranets (or 'extranets', as these networks are called when intranets are brought together to connect split-site operations and suppliers across continents), maybe with different parts of the world leading different parts of your global strategy. Astra Zeneca does this with its centres of excellence dispersed around the globe. So, you can indeed be everywhere at the same time.

Small is the new big

And, of course, if you are a centre of excellence yourself, you don't have to be part of a big organization. 'I buy my wine from a local South African vineyard I found on the Net,' says Network member Dave Allen, Global CEO of Enterprise IG, who is based in London, England. 'I have an email conversation with the owner. My wine arrives about ten days later. About five people run this business out of Stellenbosch. The *New York Times* just voted their Cabernet Sauvignon wine of the year. How can these five people communicate with me from thousands of miles away like I'm their only customer, but my globally-aspirational bank down the road still hasn't a clue how to approach me?'

We all have a lot to learn from small businesses about how to become the local supplier to someone thousands of miles away. Not only do you need to re-think 'global', but re-think 'local'. They are no longer opposites. They can be the same thing. You can picture someone like Dave Allen re-configuring his world of local suppliers from being physically based in his neighbourhood – the old definition of local – to a collection of local-minded suppliers, ranging from his winemaker in Stellenbosch to a fishmonger on the northern coast of Scotland to a tailor in the suburbs of Delhi.

You don't have to be American Express's size to operate globally. Globalism can live in small places, too. But, if you *are* AmEx's size, you'll need a strategy. Here's their global corporate travel service strategy, as an example of how to construct one.

AmEx's three-level globalism

How does one of the Top 5 most recognized brands in the world
and one of the 15 most valuable stay afloat in the new global soup?
American Express's Bernard Harrop explains the company's three-tier
approach to doing business globally with corporate customers:

Travel is corned beef

'Travel is increasingly a commodity product, rather than the emotional
purchase it was. The transparency of the Net, the ability to search and
find, is largely responsible. It's the old disintermediation thing. Travel
becomes corned beef. So, how do you create value in that context?'

What Amex corporate customers want

'… was our start point. Our research told us they wanted to cut the
costs of their travel budget, increase their own control over it, leverage supplier relationships and operate in a more global environment
without compromising service.'

The answer is Three

'In response to this customer need, AmEx is building a global network
of linked data. The system has a three-tiered architecture, like so …'

Level One: Local offices

'A local presence gives you a platform to deliver local best prices and
relationship management.'

Level Two: Regional

'In travel, regions are increasingly seen as single markets. So, AmEx has
built a regional network as a middle layer.'

Level Three: Global

'A global network of linked data gives corporate clients access to local
best prices combined with the ability to control spend and leverage
supplier relationships.'

'To hold the three-tier system together, the functional heads of the global divisions at the top are still part of local teams in the area where they are based. So, there is the flexibility for small customers to stay local, but for bigger customers to get regional and even global support depending on the scale and nature of their needs.'

Follow the sun
'There is no night-time in AmEx's world. Wherever you call from, even at 4am, the call is received in part of the world where it is still office hours. All call centres have their information linked globally and an individual caller's file is accessed by whichever centre is open and taking calls. This "follow the sun" route to offering global service that never closes, was pioneered by IT support companies. It's why AmEx's centre in Nice, France, speaks 15 languages. And it's why an AmEx call centre was set up in Brighton, on the UK's south coast – because of the surfeit of European-speaking students based there who serve as a recruitment pool.

'The system is still under development but offers some pointers for other world players who have to reconcile global with local. *Glocal* was the word coined in the mid 1990s to describe the end-state that large corporations were fumbling towards at that time. AmEx's three-tier system is one of the more successful attempts to get close to a glocal solution.'

Walls or windows
'When the wind of change blows, some build walls, some build windows', says Bernard. 'In the US, they have introduced a bill to prevent government jobs going offshore. Do you care where things are made or done? If so, you are applying old-think to your business model. Do you see globalism as hero or villain? The jury's out. But, it is up to all of us to pull it in the direction of hero with the global systems and practices we put in place.'

Source: AmEx Europe's Bernard Harrop.

So much for an example of global restructuring. How about globalizing your leaders? Professor Jonathan Gosling of Exeter University offers an interesting take on how to develop yourself and your fellow leaders to lead from a global rather than a partial perspective. Jonathan took a bunch of what he terms 'post-modern business leaders' to Sarajevo to engage them with the real world and help in the rebuilding of the administration there directly after the Yugoslav war. He is a great proponent of immersing your would-be global leaders in the complexities of the world in this way rather than letting them skate their way across the world's surface. Here's what he told us:

The post-modern, international leader

'There's a new generation of international technocrats who come pr loaded with MBAs and cross-functional, cross-border experience ar can provide textbook answers to any situation or country you throw them into. The question is: how do you develop them to deal with the new world order in an inspired rather than textbook way?

The population of leaders in your organization probably:

1   is highly-educated;
2   has cross-functional, often cross-country experience. They are no longer silo thinkers;
3   has been through a number of organizations (and re-organizations);
4   has traversed generations of technology; and
5   has been through the personal leadership development programmes.

These post-modern leaders tend to have strong habits of generalization, quickly identifying problems generically like "not getting close enough to the customer" or "poorly-managed supply chain." They're sharp-shooters: they can identify and categorize a problem from 100 yards away.

They're globetrotters who see a blur of difference instead of a plurality of world views. The consequences of their decisions are generally not visited upon them because these jet-set leaders move on so fast'.

So what do you do with them?

'You need to do three things with them:

1   *FOCUS* them on the work people are actually doing instead of stand-ins or proxies like shareholder value, efficiency and other generics, all of which are important but peripheral.

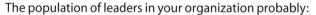

2   Get them to *OBSERVE* how leadership achieves things instead of seeing leadership as a list of competencies. "You can observe a lot by watching", as the baseball coach Yogi Berra famously said.

3   Develop *DELIBERATIVE SKILLS*. Expose and evaluate their value judgements and ability to make decisions that fit practical examples. At the aerospace company BAe, how you fix an aircraft undercarriage is part of the build and maintenance of planes. That's complicated. But it has right and wrong answers that don't make you a great leader. How you bring up your kids is an example of deliberative skills that are far more difficult'.

Jonathan Gosling, Professor of Leadership Studies, Exeter University, UK

No more fries with that?

In one very clear sense, the 21st century will not and cannot be another *American Century*. Extending across borders to engage in business globally will take more than saturating the American home market, then rolling out the same standard brand to the rest of the world, using the methods that worked in the US. This was 20th century Americanism, in which Coke and rock 'n' roll effortlessly conquered the rest of the world simply because they were born in the USA.

But, it's not so simple now. The UK Chancellor (at time of writing), Gordon Brown, has an anecdote he tells about a Group of Nine summit (G9, bringing together ministers from the major economies in the world). Looking out of his hotel window, he saw a banner draped across a building by protesters. It read

'The worldwide movement against globalization'

Some members of our Network (usually the American members, it must be said) argue that the backlash against globalism is a backlash against homogenization, not against Americanism, if we define the latter as the US exporting its brand of business around the world. Consumers are rebelling against bland templates imposed from afar that lack personal and local connections. The targets they choose just happen to be mostly American.

But these same Network members do concede that there is a global competence problem among CEOs today, many of whom are, in fact, American. Global competence was not a part of the job requirement when many of the longer-standing US CEOs currently in place were hired, which is a lesson for all of us now doing business in a small world. Alysson Stewart-Allen has spent years defining traditional Americanism. Here's what she told us:

AMERICANISM IN BUSINESS DEFINED

7 'soft exports' from the US of A

1   *An 'anything's possible' attitude.* Even Post-it Notes and three-legged tights, sorry, pantyhose (the third leg is a replacement you can step into if you ladder one of the other two – see http://www.totallyabsurd.com).

2   *A general intolerance* of companies/countries that don't do business 'the American way' (see points 3–7 for the American way of doing business).

3   *A Darwinian approach* to business competition.

4   *Win-win.* Doing business with partners in a way that makes all sides feel they have benefited [*Authors' note*: Hmmmm…if you say so].

5   *Insularity.* When your nation covers six time zones and they stopped teaching geography as a required subject back in the 1970s, it's inevitable.

6   *Valuing the individual* over the group: doesn't help when it comes to integrating and meshing with local communities.

7   *Low-context communication.* A lack of undercurrents or hidden agenda. What Americans say tends to be what you get.

Alysson Stewart-Allen, the (American) author of
Working With Americans

If you're an American business leader, or work with some, our advice is that Americanism needs to do three things to adapt:

1   Look, think and act local.

2   Integrate. Arbitrage. Cross-pollinate (rather than imposing an existing model).

3   Export the best of your corporate culture on a market-by-market basis, learning as you go, rather than using the cookie-cutter (one size fits all) approach.

And don't forget your roots. If you re-visit how you began to grow in the States, there are pointers for how you grow globally. Expanding from a position of success in one continent to another can lead to resistance; can be perceived as arrogance, as imperialism. Re-defining yourself as the global equivalent of a start-up, by reminding yourself of how you started in your home market, can bring more acceptance from the territories you now want to do business with.

Here's an example of what we mean. McDonald's botched the launch of its Swiss business because the Swiss all came in and sat down and waited to be served at the table. Long wait that would be, then. Our Network member Andrew Fraser went back to McDonald's earliest advertising in the US and found it had said: 'Come to the counter for good food, a smile and change out of a dollar'. Ray Croc and his fellow Golden Arches pioneers had educated their home market originally. But, it was so long ago, his successors had forgotten the need to go through that stage when rolling out to the rest of the world.

McDonald's gets it

McDonald's is perceived as the icon of American imperialism, rolling out a homogenized product and forcing Big Macs into the world's open mouths. But, the truth is, the Golden Arches (though, at time of writing, McDonald's is said to be looking at abandoning this global icon) have been practising localization for years, adapting menus to local preference. McDonald's most successful expansion market in 2003, where they were opening on average a restaurant every six days, and where its franchises are most profitable, is … France. Yes, the country that is the most accepting of all things American, most welcoming of foreign cuisine.

We mentioned above, when taking a look at American Express's global structure, that the 1990s saw the emergence of glocalism as the notional solution to the risk of cultural rejection. This is the strategy McDonald's has experimented with in recent years, to deal with the capacity problem – the fact that there are only so many hamburgers the world can eat and we are approaching that saturation point. The clumsy fusion word 'glocal' was shorthand for the idea that the future of business was said to be a global presence with a local flavour.

We are the world

There is still a big question here about the American psyche; whether American producers have a global positioning system in their heads that locates themselves as sufficiently *of* this planet to move onto new ways of doing business in it. We're not talking here about the alarmingly high percentage of American citizens who claim to have been abducted by aliens and then returned to earth (3.7 million according to Anita Roddick in her book *Numbers*). We're talking about how, when you're in the heart of God's own country, with a thousand miles to the ocean, the rest of the world can become a speck on the horizon of your consciousness. Therefore, designing for and doing business with people outside your borders who are, in the language of US Immigration, aliens, can so easily become an exercise in failing to connect.

There are some promising signs of a shift in mindset and practice that came through experimentation with glocalism through the 1990s. Whirlpool Corporation's 'World Washer' of 1992 was a global washing machine, destined for India, Mexico and Brazil. But, it ended up as three different versions. The Indian one had to be re-designed, because it couldn't cope with eighteen-foot long saris. And the Brazilian model had to have a special soak cycle built in, because Brazilians, according to local research, feel that clothes that haven't soaked haven't been washed properly.

In the 1990s, when Ford finally (after decades of fitfully trying) succeeded in creating a world car to sell on both sides of the Atlantic, it did so by using European as well as US designers. The car was called in Europe, the Mondeo, celebrating its world car status. Not in the US, though, where the word Mondeo had no meaning. The notion of glocalism has been refined further in recent years, particularly by the bank HSBC, which practises what it calls multi-localism. It uses an incredibly complicated but effective kit of parts to brand itself differently around the world as 'The world's local bank'.

Which raises the question for you and your global brand – if you have one or aspire to have one – where do you go next? And what are the pitfalls to avoid as you lead your brand into this strange new world? Dave Allen, CEO, Enterprise IG, runs the global branding arm of Martin Sorrell's WPP, the advertising and marketing group which is itself as global as you can get. Who better to brief us on the strange goings on in the world of global brands, including why you can't buy Heinz ketchup in Poland and why the Truth will set you free …

The Inspired Leader's short history of global brands, including what happens next

Where do global brands come from?

'From countries, paradoxically. The great global brands are commonly rooted in a country of origin. People are comforted to know that Mercedes has German engineering behind it. Harley-Davidson is the embodiment of the American dream. Many of the great global brands have a country in their name – BBC, Bank of America …'

Embarrassed by nationality

'… But in the 1990s, UK companies began to ask our advice about dropping the 'British'. The BTs and BAs felt that being rooted in a country would hinder their ability to take the global opportunity. Not necessarily so. Countries have their own brand attributes that can be built on. Japanese companies own the quality and reliability space. So much so that a UK high street electronic stores chain invented a Japanese-sounding brand to create the illusion of quality.'

Then something strange happened

'Instead of emerging from countries, competition started to emerge from the strangest places. If you'd said to me a few years back that one of the biggest threats to Coke would come from religious groups I'd have laughed. Then along came Qibla Cola and Mecca Cola, which sell millions of cases and can't be manufactured fast enough to meet demand.

And the biggest threat to Unilever's profits emerged from a diet plan formulated by Dr Atkins.'

NGOs* impact on brands

(*Non-Governmental Organizations.) 'When Greenpeace occupied BP rigs, I talked to John Brown *(BP CEO and a client of Dave's)* about not suing them, but going to talk to them instead. He met them. The dialogue profoundly affected him and led him to change how he said BP should operate. Same with Shell and Brent Spar. The Berlin Wall wasn't the only one coming down in that period.'

The answer is chocolate

... as it so often is. 'Who'd have thought organic foods and good employment practices would be what made customers decide to buy from you? Green & Black's organic chocolate is the perfect example of an emerging brand that re-defines "global" from meaning geographical reach through sales, to meaning "being of the world".' The Fair Trade movement more generally is a broader example of this new interpretation of global business – connecting people across the world based on a shared sense of fairness, represented in the company's sourcing policy and the values it expresses.

So, global or local?

'Both, probably. For every company trying to create a global brand there are as many trying to build a strong local one. Some, like SAB Miller the brewers, have a portfolio of local brands with a couple of global brands, too. Eastern Europe is not responding well to US brands, so Heinz bought a local ketchup brand in Poland called *Pudliszki* and markets its ketchup under that brand. Cadbury's did the same, marketing its products as *Wedel* chocolate in Poland.'

What's that up ahead? Looks like the truth

'Where is all this branding heading? The Truth, is my theory. This is the first time I've tested it in public. There is pent-up human frustration with brands that are not totally truthful.'

If your brand is to be rooted in the truth

' ... it means you have to:
1   Be rooted in real values.
2   Be more aware of all social groups and respectful of their needs.
3   Have employees who are properly informed and involved.

4   Above all, act with great integrity.'

How do you build integrity into a global brand?
1   'Use values to drive behaviours.
2   Strive to align image with reality.
3   Build complete buy-in – learn to behave like the UN, where everyone has to buy-in (!)
4   Believe competition can come from anywhere.
5   Think outside the country box.'

SOURCE: Dave Allen, briefing a gathering of the Inspired Leaders Network in a session at the UK's Treasury. Dave is the acknowledged master of global branding. He grew Enterprise IG, WPP's global branding arm, from a tiny office in Covent Garden, central London, to a global organization with offices in 26 countries and 750 staff.

World of contrasts

The new world of globalism is also a world of plenty. Possibly for the first time, the world is producing more things than it can consume. That's one ingredient in the new global soup. Yet, like that William Gibson comment at the start of this book ('The future is already here. It's just not evenly distributed'), neither, obviously, is the plenty. You don't have to go from Manhattan to Sao Paolo to discover the contrasts. Sometimes from one end of the street to the other will do it.

The statistics are salutary:

- Every European cow is subsidised to the value of US $2.50 a day.
- Yet, three billion humans live on less than $2 a day.
- 20% of the world's population consumes 86% of the world's resources.[5]

What does this have to do with your business and how you lead? Your employees, customers and business partners are increasingly aware of global inequity and it makes them/us uneasy. An increasing proportion of them want to know what you are doing to shoulder your corporate governance responsibilities before trusting you enough to do business with you or wanting to work for you. Which is why we see Utopian wording appearing in the corporate purpose or mission statements of giant corporations. Unilever's Corporate Purpose, for example, includes this: 'We believe that to succeed requires the highest standards of Corporate Behaviour towards our Employees, Consumers and the Societies and World in which we live.'

Fine words.

Business in a connected world

So, the world is no longer shaped as it was. The key secret that inspired leaders apply to leading their business in this new landscape is to abandon the comfort of old nation-based ideas such as import/export, country managers and rolling out a standard product globally. Instead, they discover new commercial opportunities by re-thinking their perspective and by taking account of a powerful lobby calling for a more equitable approach to world business.

As a final thought for this chapter, if you still think global inequity has nothing to do with how you lead your business …

One of the authors was a guest at an internal Andersen Consulting event (shortly before they became Accenture) and the surprise speaker was Bob Geldof, the sometime rock star, organizer of Band Aid and a successful businessman in his own right. Here's an extract from the paper Sir Bob delivered to several hundred of the highest-paid business consultants in the world, and a good number of leaders from their multi-national client companies. It's compelling stuff:

'This is a connected world. I have been in virtual meetings with our programmers, with them talking to me from the Indian sub-continent and me talking to them from my home in London, with my kids climbing all over me. End-customers are no longer just consumers. They feel connected to the problems of the developing world. And, if you have any sense, you will reflect that concern in your business dealings. If you think you can carry on with business as usual and ignore the fact that there are people starving in parts of the world or being exploited in sweatshops as part of your supply chain as if it lacks relevance, then who the Hell do you think you are? Where do you get that arrogance from? Your customers and the other people you deal with care. You do not have the right to ignore unpalatable things as if they have nothing to do with you and your business."[6]

This chapter drew on the thinking and practices of the following friends and members of the Inspired Leaders Network:

Andrew Fraser
Formerly Chief Executive of Invest UK, the head of inward investment for the UK Government. Now, Senior Advisor, Mitsubishi.

Anita Roddick
Founder, The Body Shop.

John Plender
Columnist, *Financial Times*.

Frank Nigriello
Head of Advanced Learning Systems, Unipart.

Mary Jo Jacobi
Former White House Advisor. Now VP, Group External Affairs, Royal Dutch/Shell Group.

Professor Jonathan Gosling
Director of Leadership Studies, Exeter University.

Alysson Stewart-Allen
Director, International Marketing Partners, author, *Working With Americans*.

Bernard Harrop
Director, Corporate Services, Industry Affairs, American Express Europe Ltd.

David Grayson CBE
Director, Business In The Community.

Dave Allen
Global CEO, Enterprise IG (WPP's global branding arm).

The impossible isn't

This chapter in 30 seconds

Who remembers Alexander the Average? 'The impossible' is just something that hasn't been done in your sector yet. Or even imagined. Like elephants crossing mountains. So, who's going to do it; you or someone else?

Learning how to paint a step-change picture is key to achieving break-throughs. Martin Luther King didn't say, 'I have a critical path schedule'. You also have to rethink risk and reality. Dare: do build castles in the air. Then build the foundations from the ground up. Bring a tiger into the room if you have to convince people your impossible vision is possible. And don't make the dumb mistake of not following through; give your people permission to break old rules to achieve new goals.

'The modules are austere and haphazardly put together, the whole city/castle hangs precariously from the smoothness that supports it, and nothing ever gets done as intended. But the view! The view more than compensates for the dangers and discomfort. They are pioneers, explorers of a whole new world extending in all directions outwards. The air is clear, the sun shines with intense brilliance from the deep blue sky and the clouds drift by in ever-new permutations. Isn't it worth the sacrifice of safety and protection to be a part of this?'

Anders Sandberg

The impossible isn't

> 'On the surface I am an average person,
> But to my heart I am not an average person,
> To my heart, I am a great moment.
> The challenge I face is how to dedicate everything I have inside me
> To fulfilling this moment.'
>
> *Abraham Herschel, 1965*
>
> 'Nearly everyone takes the limits of his own vision for the limits of
> the world. A few do not. (Join them.)'
>
> *Arthur Schopenhauer* [1]

If not you, then who?

When President Kennedy announced that America would put a man on the moon before the end of the decade, his scientific advisers gave him a barrage of reasons why it was impossible. What he was promising simply couldn't be done. One reason was that no fuel existed that could do the job. Kennedy switched the context from, 'It can't be done because the fuel doesn't exist', (a context of impossibility) to, 'Then, if that is where we need to stretch, go create a fuel that will do the job.' And they did.

In doing so, America's space scientists created a whole new branch of chemistry – boron chemistry – which a young science undergraduate called Mike Harris later studied at university. Mike went on to become the founding CEO of the world's first telephone-only bank, First Direct. He also headed up Mercury, the first competitor to take on British Telecom when the UK telecommunications market was deregulated. And he co-founded and currently helps to lead Egg, the pioneering digital bank. Mike told the Kennedy story in one of our Network sessions.

> '**We move because we hate the idea of standing still.**
> **We create because we want something new in our life.**
> **We take the next step because we want to rise above.**
> **This is our mission, this is our passion.**'
>
> *Daewoo Corporation*

Your one paragraph primer

Mike's one paragraph answer when asked how he consistently broke sectoral assumptions to create something new at First Direct, Mercury and then Egg, echoes the Kennedy anecdote above: 'Starting from your commitment to an unreasonable result – the "impossible achievement" that you have set out to achieve – analyze what you already have (resources, people etc.), quantify the gap between that and what you need to achieve the goal, then work out how to fill the gap.'

So far this sounds like the sculptor Auguste Rodin's supposed response when asked to explain how he made his marble horses so incredibly lifelike:

> '**Find a large piece of marble.**
> **Take a hammer and chisel.**
> **Cut away everything that doesn't look like a horse.**'

To take First Direct to market in a whirlwind nine months, Mike had scoured the world for new leadership approaches that could get him there. He has since found four, which he still recommends today:

- *dialogue* (Mike recommends the book *On Dialogue*, David Bohm, Lee Nichol (Ed.) Routledge 1996);
- *the science of complexity* ;[2]
- *system dynamics* (a mathematical modelling system developed at the Massachusetts Institute of Technology: you use it to model the strategies of all participants in a sector;[3] and
- Tracy Goss's work – called the Re-Invention Methodology for 'Making the Impossible Happen' – on *transformational change* for leaders and their organizations.[4]

The starting principle for making impossible-type changes that emerges from Mike's research is illustrated by the Kennedy anecdote, above: 'Don't ever start from a position of trying to fix the organization. You don't drive major change by saying, "What's wrong with this is …" You drive it by saying, "What's missing, which we need to create before we can achieve this, is …" Your strategy and action plan come from your conditions.'

Mind over matter

Often, the conclusion that something is impossible comes from accepting the assumptions in which your sector's current practices are rooted. Those assumptions often come tumbling down when you challenge them. Egg launched an internet-only credit card, for example. The industry's assumption was that a profitable internet-only credit card was not possible. 'The assumption was that bad debts would kill it. But Egg's card has one of the lowest customer default rates in the world. The myth that this was impossible had arisen because a couple of US banks had experimented with badly-controlled, sub prime lending when they launched the first Net cards a couple of years previously.

Our Network member Charles Dunstone, the founder of the Carphone Warehouse, points out that nobody had broken the four-minute mile until Roger Bannister did. Then the 'impossible' barrier that had stood for as long as records had been kept was trampled underfoot by Chris Brasher and a hundred other runners who, in the few years after Bannister's achievement, did it too. The distance remained the same. Time hadn't obligingly slowed down to let them cover the mile in less than four minutes. All that had changed was their understanding of what was possible and what was not. Bannister had broken the rules that were limiting them. 'Rules are for people who aren't willing to invent their own', noted another speedy human, Chuck Yeager, the first man to break the sound barrier.

In basketball, Michael Jordan leapt so far and so high and with such soaring grace that he appeared to have developed the ability to hang in the air. An urban legend spread that he could fly. It wasn't actually believed, but it spread anyway because, well, it was one way of describing what people were seeing that they couldn't otherwise describe. Today, thanks to Jordan, you can see miracles happening on every street corner. Kids playing basketball on municipal courts from Brooklyn on the east coast to Oakland on the west, regularly sail through the air with the same loping, arm-extended, trademark slow-mo leaps that seem to go on forever, making you stop and believe, for a fraction of a second, that they are indeed flying. It's not the *Nike Air Jordan* shoes that give them wings. They can do it because Michael Jordan himself showed them it was possible.

If your sector's rules define something as impossible, make your own rules

'We were the first to fit cardiac defibrillators on our aircraft and train our crews how to use them. The medical and legal profession strongly advised against it. But Richard (Branson) insisted on it. The first time we used it, at 35,000 feet, it was on a passenger who technically "died" four times. Our staff, and the defibrillator, saved him. Now, all full-service airlines carry a defibrillator and train their staff in how to use it.

'It's a crime of the first order, in Richard's eyes, to be "me too". That's why we created drive-thru check-ins, challenging the convention that said you had to queue to check in hand luggage. It was based on the realization that our Upper Class passengers were time poor.

'So we developed it as an extension of our free limo pick-up service, allowing Upper Class passengers to check in from the back of the limo. The driver calls ahead. The passenger gives the

driver their ticket and boarding pass and checks in while reading
their *FT* or whatever in the back of the car.

'Malcolm McLaren, the legendary manager of the Sex Pistols,
said, "There are two ways to lead your life: karaoke (copying) or
authenticity." Copy or break the mould. That's the choice you face
every day. The phrase "first-mover advantage" is usually applied
to the internet. Apply it to everything. Make it part of your organization's broader mindset; a refusal to play by someone else's
rules. It's your people who create these service innovations. Really
clever service types will see through their customers' eyes.'

Lyell Strambi, Chief Operating Officer, Virgin Atlantic

So, encouraging people to challenge sectoral assumptions and
think the impossible is an obvious prerequisite before you and
your people can actually *do* the impossible. That's the mindset part
that Lyell Strambi talks about in the example above – encouraging a culture of 'it doesn't have to be this way' thinking. It's the
parameters or perceived rules around the way things are done
now that categorize an alternative action as impossible. The definition of 'check-in' is hemmed around with these parameters: you
stand in line, you check in personally, the check-in desk is in the
terminal building, you manhandle your own luggage into a cart
with a wobbly wheel, you don't know what to do with the cart
once your luggage has gone through, you get to stand in a shorter
line if you're a First Class passenger …

But, someone at Virgin decided to ignore that definition and
come up with another one; one that had new parameters around
it that suddenly made the impossible possible – checking in from
the back of a car, no cart, kicking back, reading the newspaper or
drinking coffee – as long as you were an Upper Class passenger, of
course.

Take the blue pill

… or the red pill. To achieve extraordinary results on a regular
basis, you may need to alter your reality. No drugs involved. Promise. The 'red pill or blue pill' analogy is from the movie *The Matrix*,
in which the main character is offered a pill that will allow him to

'see' reality for what it *really* is or one that will allow him to sink back into his artificial reality. A surprising number prefer not to see what's really out there.

The irrational exuberance of the late 1990s left the business world a more cautious place. Timidity has reigned for a number of years now; a wariness that trying to create a business out of something you can't see is a foolish thing. Talk of achieving the impossible scares off some leaders who want to stay rooted in reality. It's true that *confronting reality*, as Larry Bossidy and Ram Charan remind us in their book of the same name,[5] is what leaders have to do all the time.

And we recommend it. Not enough leaders do it. 'Be real' is one of the silent screams that goes on inside all of us when faced with a corporate world of spin and plastic inauthenticity. But that doesn't mean be boring or predictable. There's room for at least some rational exuberance, don't you think? There is no contradiction between being real and reaching for the impossible. In fact, you can't have one without the other. If your castles in the air aren't rooted in foundations built from the ground up, they will fall spectacularly to earth. Enron. Dotcom boom. Say no more.

There are mental tricks you can encourage to help develop an ability to see alternative realities, to break free of the assumptions that limit possibilities. We mentioned them in passing in the chapter on leading innovation. Edward De Bono tells a fascinating story that illustrates one approach: asking yourself impossible questions, and encouraging your people to ask themselves and each other impossible questions, too.

Ask impossible questions

De Bono tells the true tale of Ron Barbaro of Prudential Canada,[6] who was driving home after visiting a terminally ill friend. 'His life insurance is useless at the moment, since it's not unlocked until he dies. So, how can you die before you die?' is the 'impossible' question that kept running around Barbaro's head, prompted by his friend's plight.

Barbaro solved the impossible question by changing the rules, creating a new form of product called Living Needs Benefit, which pays out before death. Now every major life company offers a Living Needs Benefit-type policy. It was that impossible question, 'How can you die before you die?' that led to the breakthrough. Once again, the best answer destroys the question. It was a pretty good career move, too; Barbaro went on to become president of the company. But, just thinking the impossible is not enough. Action springs not just from thought, but from a readiness for responsibility, Dietrich Bonhoeffer observed. Add that to imagination and you've reconciled the unreal with the real: you've got the formula for creating a new reality, for achieving the 'impossible'.

Imagination and action

One of the authors took the family to Disneyland Paris. In the brochure it said it would snow each night. Not a big, fanfare announcement; just a single line of type buried in the brochure. And it did snow. But, when the author's son, Danny, pointed upward to the Paris night sky at tiny flecks of snow swirling around Main Street, it still took us all by surprise. Because it wasn't snowing anywhere else in Paris. In fact, it wasn't snowing anywhere else but in Main Street, as we discovered by running into other parts of the park then running back. We made a bit of a spectacle of ourselves by jumping up and down trying to catch a snowflake, to see how they did it. We caught one, and it lasted less than a second in a cupped hand, before disappearing, as you'd expect a snowflake to.

But, less than a second was just enough time for us to spot that the snowflake was not snow; it was a cluster of tiny bubbles that had been designed by a Disney *imagineer* to look and act like snow. So, somewhere in the rooftops were hidden bubble machines spraying out customized bubbles that had been specially designed to act like small snowflakes, for fifteen minutes each night. Like Disney's imagineers, your people clearly need the power to act on their imagination if you are to deliver miracles like snow-on-demand.

Our Network member Kris Murrin tells a great story about how one of Disney's imagineers used action to achieve a breakthrough. This imagineer had twice presented to the Disney board a thick, bound proposal for a new park that featured live animals, she says.

Twice, the proposal was thrown out on the grounds that 'people don't want to see live animals. Where's the "wow" in that?' The third time, the imagineer didn't bring a thick proposal into the boardroom with him. He brought in, on the end of a chain, a six-foot Bengal tiger. 'Now do you get it?' he asked. They got it. Disney's Animal Kingdom was the result.[7]

Coping with complexity

The complexity and unpredictability of fast-moving markets can get in the way of your attempts to challenge reality and define your impossible dream, let alone make it real. Fake snow is an operational creation of a small miracle. But, it's only a small miracle. Mike Harris points out that at strategic level you need to maintain clarity to achieve the apparently impossible, and maintaining clarity when markets appear chaotic and increasingly interconnected can, of itself, seem an impossible task.

'A definition of complexity might be any number of issues, interpreted differently by each person, and all interconnected. More and more interconnectedness creates a complexity that is difficult to grasp', Mike told us. 'At Egg, we defined 321 issues that needed to be addressed, each with up to 40 different interpretations. Using a computer-aided dialogue tool, we reduced these to three things that really mattered. It was the most successful intervention I can recall in terms of producing defined actions at speed in unpredictable circumstances.'

Looking back at First Direct (which has consistently maintained, ever since it was started more than fifteen years ago, the highest customer satisfaction and customer referral rating of any bank in the UK), Mike says that the key to its extraordinary development was 'that we managed to set a "shared context", which enabled the group to reach heroic achievements. It is a science-based theory, observable when a group becomes capable of more intelligent results than the sum of its parts. If you can set a shared context, everyone knows where you are coming from, they come to believe that the target is achievable, however impossible it seemed initially. The vision is not a remote target in the future; it is current and available now. There is less need for controls because they share the vision and understand the context.

'How do you set a shared context? First it must be defined. The leader should facilitate its development, by talking, listening, responding; drawing in all aspects, all contributions, creating the agenda. Open to all contributions, leaders should not be attached to their own opinions ... '

(*PAUSE*. Yes, you read that correctly. If you glided by it, stop and go back and let the significance sink in. Leaders should not be attached to their own opinions. You don't necessarily have the right answers. Prevailing is not what leadership is about ... *CONTINUE*).

'Other qualities include toleration of creativity and experimentation – that is the way to move forward; define how much you are going to tolerate. Do not show discouragement at any time, and deal with it in staff before dealing with the problem. Realize that every gesture by a leader has an impact, a dramatic effect.'

Fire and ice

Mike also recommends the work of David Whyte, a poet, in understanding the conflicting feelings that your people (and indeed you) have to deal with when you challenge them to take on impossible changes. Whyte uses images of fire and ice to illustrate his management theory. 'Fire is current, compelling, exciting – the creative spark. You need to fire people up with your vision because the passion it generates gets people enrolled. By defining the big game you can draw people in, stoke up the heat', says Mike. 'But, as humans we are contradictory, and we fear being burned. So we think of ice as securing us against risk. Ice represents caution, but ice extinguishes creativity and freezes action.'[8]

'Leaders need to work on themselves too, to assess themselves constantly. How do you deal with threats? Do you reveal disappointment, discouragement, or freeze with fear? Dialogue is so important here. If the context is shared, you will get innovation, the team working together. Know that you, too, are being held to account by the team.

'In a start-up, you have nothing; it is hard work setting a shared context when you have nothing there. In a legacy business, you have to work differently. Key is the need to thoroughly understand the business, what is driving it. Then you have to introduce new possibilities and dialogue continuously, for as long as it takes. Don't criticize, because that entrenches opposition. And focus relentless on the vision, on what you are creating, or the legacy culture will kill you off.'[9]

Mike Harris

Bend it like Beckham

Modern-day athletes use visualization to picture impossible outcomes, incidentally. You should try it, too. England footballer (soccer player, that is) David Beckham is famous for banana-curve free kicks whipped into the goal from distance with such power and precision that (when they work) they seem to defy the laws of physics. He mentally rehearses a kick by picking the spot in the goal that he wants to hit, then repeatedly 'sees' the flight of the ball – its trajectory and the velocity he needs to achieve to pass the goalkeeper – before stepping up to kick it for real. Mind over matter.

'The vision thing' as George Bush, senior, so memorably and dismissively called it, definitely seems to be essential to breakthrough thinking and action. But only if it *is* definite. Keeping that vision real, distinct and achievable and linked to people's work, not distant and generic, is the key to performing organizational mind over matter. If you want to bend it like Beckham you have to mentally rehearse repeatedly those steps that turn vision into reality. Our Network member John O'Keeffe has researched this and come up with eight paths for moving from step-by-step incremental actions to organizational habits that enable you and your team to practise breakthrough thinking and action.

8 paths from incremental habits to – > breakthrough habits

1   Happy doing a bit better – > Picture a step-change
2   Drown in information – > Build knowledge
3   Logic alone – > Use creativity as a business weapon
4   Think, then act – > Think in the action zone (collapse the two)
5   Half-brained organization – > Whole-brained (add gut and instinct)
6   Trapped by limited mindsets – > Powered by 'what if?' mindsets
7   Meetings & memos – > Hats, maps and thinking pads
8   Grit your teeth and push on – > Set yourself on fire and recharge.

Inspired Leader *John O'Keeffe*, former Group VP, Procter & Gamble

'Learning how to paint a step-change picture is key to achieving those stretch goals that large corporations like to set themselves to shake off complacency', says John. 'Martin Luther King didn't say, "I have a critical path schedule". Moreover, as he urged people towards his dream, he also told them what to move away from. He understood that incrementalism was inhibiting because people would become satisfied with seeing small changes as progress. And, so he used a provocative word picture to get this message across. Words can help you avoid the tranquillizing drug of gradualism.'

Here are two examples, first quoted by Poras & Collins:[10]

1   President Kennedy didn't announce a 'strengthening of the moon programme'. He said in 1961: 'This nation should commit itself to achieving the goal, before this decade is out, of landing a man on the moon and returning him safely to earth.' He died two years later, but his words lived on.
2   In the early 1960s, Philip Morris had only a 10 per cent market share in cigarettes – sixth in its market. It set itself a word picture to aim for: 'To become the General Motors of the tobacco industry'. And it achieved it.

A step-change goal works best when the words catch people's hearts as well as their heads, says John. Hearts are not captured by numbers, unless they are 'magic' numbers: double it, go for a million, become number one.

But, don't make the dumb mistake of not following through. Give your people permission to break old rules to achieve new goals. The worst thing you can do is set breakthrough goals and not shake up your culture to allow your people to develop break-through methods to achieve those goals. Business as usual ain't gonna get you there. Dr King's dream was accompanied by a whole raft of peaceful civil disobedience actions that outflanked the 'com-petition' – a methodology as well as a vision.

Fear of falling

Those who fail to achieve breakthroughs fail, ironically, because they engineer their overall corporate efforts to *avoid* failure or the impact of failure. In the words of the legendary ice hockey player, Wayne Gretsky,

> **'You miss 100% of the shots you don't take.'**

They appear afraid and distrustful of the people who work for them, and so constrain them with rules and hierarchy. To achieve impos-sible results, you have to let go, says our network member Rene Carayol. 'Organizations that have a reputation for changing the game, for achieving breakthroughs, have a restless energy about them that comes from the people who work within them. But, ponderous, plodding organizations are afraid to allow their people free rein, practising a control culture that ensures the energy in their people remains untapped', Rene told us.

'Those who fail to release the magic in their organizations, we find, engineer their efforts to avoid failure or the impact of failure, and thus compress their lives into what is known and predict-able. By contrast, practitioners of what we call Corporate Voodoo – the mix of new and old that will decide which companies win in the 21st century – engage fully with life and all its surprises. At bottom, it seems, slow businesses are scared of one thing more than any other: they are afraid of other human beings. The history of organizations has been the history of subjugation, control and micro-management, not because of any scientific understanding that this produces the most efficient use of the human resource, but from a deep seated fear of what might be produced without such confining approaches.'

'If things seem under control, then you're just not going fast enough.'

Mario Andretti, racing driver

Corporate magicians

But, still we come back to the difficulty of making breakthroughs when the environment in which we all operate – the markets out there – are so fluid and chaotic that the impossibility seems to lie in making sense out of the chaos, in spotting patterns and paths forward where none seem to exist. Some people turn to magicians to create order from the chaos. And sometimes it seems to work. Mike Harris says he discovered a new source of power in the executive and organizational transformation methodology created by another of our members, Tracy Goss. He put 100 or so of his top leaders through Tracy's transformation programme – Executive Re-Invention. This three week intensive programme, says Mike, was the foundation for himself and his key leaders, working in partnership with Tracy, to have 'making the impossible happen' become a core competency at Egg.

Others turn to the thinking of Fernando Flores, the Chilean magician, whose followers claim a kind of miraculous change in their organizations that is to the sterility of 1980s-style re-engineering what the magical realism tradition in South American literature is to Jane Austen. In short, electrifying. (Not that Jane Austen isn't compelling reading for many, of course …)

One of the most powerful examples of the Flores effect is Cemex, the Mexican cement company. Mexico City, in the evocative words of *Wall Street Journal* writer Thomas Petzinger, is a city of cement hills, thousands of them, blighting street corners and junctions at points all over the city. Cement, it turns out, is a perishable commodity. If you don't get to the customer in time to deliver it, you have to dump it unless you want to spend a very long time chipping it out of your delivery vehicle. The cement orders in Mexico City, where people build their own houses, are typically small and the addresses hard to find. Around 50% of Cemex's cement loads were being dumped in the chaos that was Mexico City.[11]

Learning from bees

The distribution problem was impossible to overcome. Cemex began working with the techniques of Fernando Flores, who had been the country's finance minister before being imprisoned by Pinochet when the elected government of Salvador Allende was overthrown. Flores, who is now a prominent Chilean senator again, came up with his breakthrough thinking for leading companies after spending two years in a Chilean jail cell.

Flores' people took Cemex's business design team on field trips to help them conceptualize different ways of approaching the chaotic distribution problem. They used the trips to examine how organizations faced with inescapably chaotic situations – such as 9/11 emergency response services and Federal Express – responded to their customers. They even studied the swarming algorithms of bees.

With the help of Flores' methods, Cemex redesigned how it made and delivered cement, by managing promises. Its core promise was borrowed from pizza delivery: 'We will deliver cement within half an hour of you ordering it. And if we're more than fifteen minutes late, you get it free.' That was the impossible target. By managing the commitments needed to make that happen, Cemex grew from the 7th biggest to the 2nd biggest cement company in the world. The CEO of Cemex has now been appointed to the board of IBM. Powerful stuff …

All talk, no action?

Fed up with all talk no action in your organization? You have processes for managing materials and information. The missing piece is a process for managing commitments, according to Flores. Before returning to politics, Flores frequently charged (and got) more than $1 million per project to turn around personally the leadership of large organizations by teaching them how to 'do' Commitment-Based Management. It's not an easy option. His opening pitch with one contract, a large firm based in Holland, was: 'You are assholes who know nothing ...'.[12]

'You have to be able to risk your identity for a bigger future than the present you are living', is the core of Flores' transformation philosophy that some find hard to stomach. Less open-minded executives feel there is a whiff of the Esalen Institute (that place on the Californian coast at Big Sur, right up near where all the marijuana is grown in the hills) about some of this stuff. There are echoes of rebirthing and other spiritual and emotional upheavals that are alien to most boardrooms. The apparent denigration of the existing success strategy that has got them so far holds back a number of business leaders from exploring this personal transformation route further, too: Flores used to tear down many of his clients, ripping away belief systems before building them back up again. You get a hint of what's to come in his 'assholes' opening remark to the Dutch company mentioned above.

Opinion is divided on personal transformation programmes as a route to leadership that delivers impossible results, even among the authors of this book: one of us attends sessions run by Landmark Education Corporation, which grew out of Werner Erhard's EST work; the other would rather not, thanks. It is probably this sense of having to abandon what has got them where they are so far that makes many leaders shy away from the transformation route.

Practise smart risk

Tracy Goss, however, says 'It is a misunderstanding to think that you have to start all over again and abandon everything. No-one wants to take your current success strategy – which I call your winning strategy – away from you. Choosing to operate outside your winning strategy does not mean giving it up. Being able to step outside your existing source of power gives you a new toolset for when you need it. It doesn't mean throwing the old one away.'

Mike Harris told us: 'At Egg perhaps 80% of what we do is to achieve predictable results. It's only for the 20% impossible targets that we switch to the "impossible" toolset.'

'We call it *smart risk* to distinguish what we do from the irrational exuberance that others practised in the 1990s. Yes, we set out to redefine what's possible. But we never invest more than the organization can afford to lose. The way you react to failures or disappointments is important. Does it make you less willing to take on 'impossible results'? No. You just apply the rule of smart risk: ensure that any investment you make is one you can afford to lose and that the potential success is worth the investment and risk.'

Flores's focus on the language that a leader uses to leverage radical change has been highly influential. You have processes for managing materials and information. The missing piece is a process for managing commitments. That is the sharp end of Flores' insight. With a commitment-based approach to operationalizing change, you treat discussions and meetings as 'conversations for action'. The basic action workflow is: request for action – > negotiation – > action declared complete – > request declared satisfied. Break down how your organization communicates and makes decisions and you will find at least one of those steps is missing or not agreed, according to Flores' disciples. That's the gap through which radical change slips and falls.

The promise-keepers

Billy Glennon, one of our members, leads a company that uses Flores' methods. He says the missing link in gearing yourself up to produce results previously thought impossible is *tracking promises*. 'Organizations have no systems or processes to track promises. I was explaining this to the CEO of a major banking group when he suddenly said to me, "We have seventeen call centres and I don't know what promises we make to customers, which ones we keep, which ones we miss ..." .'

People in organizations routinely sit in planning meetings making promises they know they are going to be unable to keep. But, they make them anyway. Organizations regularly set stretch targets that executives then sign up to, with each side knowing that by pretending to aim for the overambitious stretch target, they may, with a fair wind and some frantic last minute sales as the quarter closes, hit the 70% or so of the stretch target that they both knew was the real target in the first place. It's what Tom Peters means when he says, 'Ninety percent of what goes on in your organization is bullshit and you know it.'[13]

What language do you speak?

Charles Spinosa, a former Berkeley philosophy professor who works with Flores, told us that the core of the issue is the relation of the language you use in your business to action: 'Much of a manager's communication is assessments and assertions. But the four "speech acts", as we call them, that drive actions are: offers, requests, promises and declarations. Declarations, for example, can transform your reality pretty quickly, as in "You're fired", "You're hired", or "I pronounce you man and wife".

'All of us are familiar with stepping into a job, being given a complex workflow map and told "manage that". Your options for improvement are limited. You can run some activities in parallel, automate, or cut activities. But you can't innovate much. So the radical answer proposed here is to map the management conversation. Maps reveal *and* hide. Traditional activity maps don't reveal the soft stuff that causes 60% of failures. So by mapping the management conversation instead as commitment processes, you uncover the areas you need to focus on to develop new possibilities.'

Common pathologies

Whether or not you buy into the whole Flores game plan, commitment mapping is a radical tool for uncovering these kinds of pathologies within your culture:

- Listen poorly. Make vague requests.
- Predict instead of promise.
- Deliver only to specification, not to the customer's concern.
- Don't acknowledge.
- Work from the queue.
- 'I'll do my best.' (Yoda to Luke Skywalker: 'Try you say! Always trying you are! Don't try. Do!')

- Professional work ('no-one can assess or comment on my work apart from another professional').
- The executive's complaint: ('People won't take responsibility!').
- Parliament ('All talk, no action').

At time of writing, Fernando Flores, now back in the Chilean Senate as a senior politician, had pushed for a law stating that if a Chilean citizen makes a request of the state and it's not responded to within a certain timescale, it is escalated to the first secretary responsible for that area of government. If *they* then fail to respond within a certain timescale, the citizen's request is deemed to be granted. Now that's what you call a bias for action.[14]

The sixth discipline

The essential action of leaders and managers occurs almost entirely in conversations, notes the Australian leadership thinker Alan Sieler. Writing in the magazine *Management Accounting*, Synan & Black noted this:

'Peter M. Senge, in his book *The Fifth Discipline*, popularized the idea that organizations can be seen as systems with their own internal logic. Find the right way to deal with the system and it can become a "learning organization". Organizations do not learn; people learn. It may be useful to ask, "What do people do in organizations?" One of their main activities is talking. Managers spend 63–69 percent of their time in conversation. If we could develop a foundation discipline based on conversation, it might become the much sought-after sixth discipline.'[15]

To the barricades

Leading your people into an unwinnable fight, and then winning when everyone thought you were dead, is another form of impossible leadership. Say you were the incumbent running a national lottery. And say the government preferred a new consortium, being put together by none other than Richard Branson, as the lottery operator. Then the government regulator that controls the lottery tells you your company is banned from applying to run it again when your licence to do so expires. The bearded one, apparently, is going to get it. What do you do?

Start looking in the 'situations vacant' column and let the headhunters know you might be free anytime soon is the answer most business leaders would give. Not Dianne Thompson, CEO of Camelot, which runs the largest lottery in the world, the UK National Lottery. Dianne kept her nerve, took the government and Branson on, and won.

Leaders who want to achieve radical change all know about the burning platform strategy – that people won't move with you as fast as you want them to unless they have an absolutely compelling reason to do so. Creating a burning platform is always a manipulative thing to do. Being faced with a real one (well, a metaphorical one, but a real crisis) can bring forth the kind of superhuman energy you need in your people to achieve the apparently impossible; you know, as in those tales about people finding the strength to lift a car when someone is trapped under it.

Any sane leader in an apparently unwinnable situation would not take the fight to the enemy. But that's exactly what Thompson did. 'My former chairman said you could never beat Branson in the media. Yet we chose consciously to fight through the media', she told us. 'If you looked closely at our strategy, we never mentioned Sir Richard. We focused on the National Lottery Commission and made it clear our fight was with them. When journalists tried to bring it back to Branson, we said it wasn't about him. I managed to avoid mentioning him almost completely. Though once, when pressed by a journalist to admit Sir Richard could run the Lottery, I did find myself saying "I'm sure he could launch one very well …". '

Cascade communications

Thompson clearly has nerves of steel, though she says the real driving force in this situation was a burning sense of unfairness. Her company, Camelot, had been tainted in the eyes of the Commission that controlled the Lottery licence, by the inclusion among its consortium members of GTech, the lottery technology company whose practices had been found questionable in other parts of the world. Yet Camelot had taken steps to distance itself from GTech, then severed all connection with it.

It was this unfairness, said Thompson, that made her decide to fight; for her company and her people's jobs. Now this is the perfect example of the *shared context* we keep returning to in this book. There was just one agenda at Camelot: survival. Thompson introduced new practices during the crisis period, including a new communications tool. It's borrowed from those telephone chains that schools set up among parents of children on a school trip, if they have to let them all know that, say, the bus is delayed and the kids won't be back from camp for another two hours. It worked like this, Dianne told us:

'We had to communicate fast internally, because it was such a fluid situation. One fast communication tool we developed was a verbal cascade. Fourteen people are briefed by the CEO and each cascades down through a series of nominated people. There are buddies and deputy buddies for when someone is off sick or on holiday. Within 20 minutes, we reach 900 people, even our field sales people, to keep them briefed on the latest development.

I introduced it because some of our people had heard we had lost the licence – and by implication their job – on the radio before hearing it from us. They were devastated. I was determined that wasn't going to happen again. It was so successful that, even after we appealed and won, we kept it going. We still do a cascade of the previous sales figures every Monday so people know how their company is doing. It has to be person to person.'

This time it's personal

We love that 'person to person' element. Even with a workforce of almost 1,000, everyone has a personal message from the CEO passed to them by a colleague within twenty minutes. Since we observed earlier that conversation should be replacing 'communication' in the head of leaders as something they have to be good at, we should also mention here a practice introduced by another dynamic leader for sending messages up the chain to the board, to balance Dianne's cascade example of communication down the chain from the CEO.

Anita Roddick, a friend of our Network, and her husband Gordon, introduced a red letter system in their time heading up The Body Shop. Any employee with an urgent communication for the Roddicks put it in a red envelope. Anita and Gordon then dealt with the red envelope communications as an urgent item, replying within 48 hours. Richard Branson, too, is a pioneer leader when it comes to two-way communication. He issues his personal phone number to all Virgin employees and encourages them to call him with any ideas or issues they have. And they do.

Here's another caveat to add to Dianne's story: beware of becoming a crisis junkie. Being a turnaround artist is one thing. Using real or imagined crises to spur your people on to heroic achievements time after time means you are ignoring underlying systemic problems. And no doubt burning out a lot of people. Here's Mike Harris to reinforce the warning. He's describing the digital bank Egg, as it struggled to become a dotcom survivor:

Crisis junkie leadership

'One of the first things we did in our work with Tracy Goss was to reveal Egg's "Winning Strategy". As an organization our Winning Strategy was this: First we listened for what could make a massive impact on limiting or expanding our game. Second, we used that as a lever to create a crisis to rally the troops to the cause or to prevent the impending trouble, in order to (thirdly) create heroes and win by breaking the constraints. One example of our Winning Strategy in action: we hit our savings account five-year volume target in six months. The demand was about to overwhelm us. The awareness that we could go under gave us the power to sort it out and get through ... but only just. You know that feeling that 'the only time I feel really alive is in the middle of a crisis'? That was Egg.'

Mike says he broke away from crisis leadership by working with Tracy and Goss-Reid Associates to develop a cadre of leaders who could operate outside of both, their individual winning strategies, and the organization's winning strategy to drive the company forward. He told us that any leader who wants to achieve transformational change in the organization needs to see their core job as creating more leaders, taking much of the control out of their own hands and dispersing it.

We started this chapter by saying the impossible is just something no one in your sector has done yet. We'll finish it with another example to inspire you. Taking a UK car brand from the bottom to the top of the US JD Power quality charts inside five years was the impossible challenge. Ford's Sir Nick Scheele told us how he did it.

> 'You don't get your people to storm the barricades by moving your performance up from 35th to 32nd. We needed something more radical ...'
>
> *Sir Nick Scheele*

The Impossible is just something that hasn't been done in your sector yet...

A toothless Jaguar

'When Ford bought Jaguar in the early 1990s it was a mess, losing £1 million every day and 35th out of 36 brands in the JD Power rankings, based on surveying car customers. We came in just above the Yugo. As the US was 60% of our market, that wasn't a small problem. I was running Ford of Mexico when the company asked me to become Chairman of Jaguar.'

The quality problem

'Lexus, top of the rankings five years in a row, had 140 faults per 100 cars. Jaguar had 500. On my first day of touring the Browns Lane factory in the Midlands, there were cars everywhere, in various stages of rework. We clearly had a massive quality problem, directly causing the profit problem: we had a 35% loss to revenue ratio.'

Aha! Manufacturers know how to fix quality

'Yes, we threw engineers and managers at it and beat up people and processes. We improved marginally. But, it wasn't enough of a change. You don't get your people to storm the barricades by moving your performance up from 35th to 32nd. We needed something more radical.'

The impossible dream

'We had a board meeting in advance of a pay round and thrashed out how to link it to quality. We could have cut the wage bill to show how tough we were, but we knew it wouldn't bring the change needed. We asked ourselves on the board what we wanted to achieve. It was to be in the JD Power Top Three within five years.'

Re-inventing labour relations
'The answer was to break with the past and re-invent labour relations. The union expected a 10% pay cut. We offered them the cost of living plus one per cent each year. But in return, they had to lose layers of supervisors and superintendents, move to multi-skilled teamwork and take responsibility for quality.'

Changing the context
'We were saying, "You design your own jobs, decide what tools and parts you need, what measures and controls you want to use." Why? Because the root of the quality problem was that we had been asking them to punch the time clock when they came in and leave their brains at the door. Forcing quality in by engineers and managers had failed. So we handed it over to the people responsible for the work itself. They grabbed it.' (*NB This is the creation of a shared context.*)

Your car, your job, your customers ...
'That's what we told them. When a customer complaint comes in, it's followed up later with a call. We got the factory workers to make the calls. So, if someone complained about the driver's seat, one of the guys who installed the seats would be the one who called back. When we launched the XJ series around the world, in every dealership that it was launched, it was an hourly line worker from the factory who launched the car: we closed the factory for two days and sent them to the States and Europe to do it.'

The Impossible achieved
'In August 1998 I got a call from a colleague who had the latest JD Power ratings in front of him. "Are you standing or sitting, Nick?" he asked. "I'd sit down if I were you. Then listen." We had gone from 35th to 1st in the JD Power survey. We even beat Lexus.

'Leadership is about energizing people. That's how we did it. It's about changing the culture. You need to turn your pyramid upside down and see yourself as the support services for your workforce. It takes a hell of a shift in your context as a leader to be able to do this.'

Source: Ford President and COO Sir Nick Scheele, talking at an Inspired Leaders Network dinner

Start dreaming

So, inspired leaders know the impossible isn't. This chapter has given you some inspiration from our members and friends of our Network on how to take on the apparently impossible. Over to you. Start dreaming. And don't forget these two essential pieces of advice:

'Most people live in a very restricted circle of their potential being. We all have reservoirs of energy and genius to draw upon of which we do not dream.'

William James, 1899

'If you have built castles in the air your work need not be lost; that is where they should be. Now put the foundations under them.'

Henry David Thoreau

This chapter drew on the thinking and practices of the following friends and members of the Inspired Leaders Network:

Mike Harris
Executive Vice-Chairman, Egg.

Charles Dunstone
CEO, Carphone Warehouse, Europe's largest independent retailer of cellular phones.

Tracy Goss,
President, Goss-Reid Associates , Inc. Tracy is the author of *The Last Word on Power: Executive Re-Invention For Leaders Who Must Make The Impossible Happen* in which you can find out more about her transformative steps: uncovering your winning strategy, understanding the limits of the universal human paradigm, putting everything at risk, inventing a new master paradigm, inventing an impossible

game to play, breaking the addiction to interpretation, and operating beyond the limits of your winning strategy. It's powerful stuff ...

Lyell Strambi
Chief Operating Officer, Virgin Atlantic.

Kris Murrin
Partner, ?What *If!*

John O'Keeffe
Former Group VP, Procter & Gamble, author of *Business Beyond The Box: Applying Your Mind For Breakthrough Results*. John says lateral thinking is too impractical and linear thinking too inflexible. His approach to breakthroughs uses triangular thinking (you have to read the book ...).

Rene Carayol
Rene is on the board of the UK Inland Revenue, is a TV presenter, a regular columnist for *The Observer* newspaper, and charismatic conference chairman, with twenty years' experience at senior level in organizations from Pepsi to Marks & Spencer to IPC, where he sat on the main board. He is the co-author of *Corporate Voodoo*, one of our favourite books.

Billy Glennon *and* Charles Spinosa
Group CEO and Group Director respectively, Vision Consulting, which uses the techniques of Fernando Flores and teaches clients how to use them, too.

Dianne Thompson
CEO, Camelot, the UK National Lotto operator.

Anita Roddick
Founder, The Body Shop.

Sir Nick Scheele
President and COO, Ford.

Get an NBA, not an MBA

This chapter in 30 seconds

Inspired leaders architect their organizations differently. They build on founding principles. And what they build appears to be upside down and inside out compared to traditional organizations.

Technical architecture is important, of course. But this is architecture without walls: you need to learn from the spider; spin a business web that allows you to sense and respond as an organization.

The neglected area is your human or social architecture. That is where the true shape of your organization lies.

You need to rethink structure and edge and investigate cellular reproduction and other oddities as a route to growth. Who's at the top? Who's at the bottom? It's an upside down world in the architecture of an inspired organization.

If what gets measured gets done, how do you measure the soft stuff that is now the hard stuff? And what does Mick Jagger know about Knowledge Management that you don't?

Get a New Business Architecture, not an MBA

Oh no, the IT chapter!

Not entirely true.

You got this far without having to deal with too many references to IT or IS systems and there's a reason for that: Information Technology is a secondary influence on your organization's success. This isn't an anti-IT stance. It comes from Paul Strassmann, most senior of our Network's members from the IS/IT discipline. Paul is the IT economist who was the IS chief at the US Defense Department in the early 1990s and at Xerox Corp in the late 1970s and early 1980s, as well as being a senior IS adviser to NASA. He's in *CIO* (Chief Information Officer) *Magazine's* hall of fame as one of the '12 most influential CIOs of the 1990s'.

'Prowess in IT is not a competitive success factor', says Paul counter-intuitively. 'IT is a weak and secondary influence that only makes its effects visible through improving (or deteriorating) one of the primary sources of competitive success.'[1]

That doesn't mean you get to lead in an inspired way without it. It does mean that IT investment is more about keeping up with inflationary operational effectiveness thresholds than about making strategic breakthroughs. Having said that, we need to set some clear principles for how inspired leaders architect the Information Systems that feed their organizations or there will be a big IS-shaped hole in this book.

Information Systems alone will not spearhead your creation of an inspired organization. But they are necessary to facilitate it. And, if you screw up the IT, that will certainly bring your inspirational progress grinding to a halt. So, we've asked our IS big guns to give you some principles to work to in the first half of this chapter. The second half will focus on human or social architecture, so jump to that if you wish.

Come to the edge

As we've established, the edges of organizations are, increasingly, where business decisions have to be made. Traditional, pyramid-shaped organizations architected around a head office, which houses the decision makers, are now the wrong shape because markets move too quickly to wait for their decisions. Pyramids are indeed tombs.[2]

The competitive agenda has moved from decisions made at the centre to decisions made at the edge, with the context set by the centre. To be an edgy organization, you need to inspire people to lead and make decisions at all levels. That means breaking down your hierarchy and turning people around so they aren't looking upwards, hypnotized by the weight of authority looming over them. Bad leaders hide in hierarchies. They cling to them, like scaffolding, to maintain their elevated position. And they insist on being looked up to. As Jack Welch so memorably put it, *'Hierarchy is an organization with its face to the boss and its ass to the customer.'*[3]

> **'Leadership is about energizing people ... You need to turn your pyramid upside down and see yourself as the support services for your workforce. It takes a hell of a shift in your own context – your sense of what it is to be a leader – to be able to do this.'**
> *Sir Nick Scheele, President, Ford Motor Company, speaking at an Inspired Leaders Network midsummer dinner.*

Inspired leaders re-architect their organizations. We'll start here with a few words of guidance from the IS and IT leaders among our

Network on some of the principles you need to apply (or ensure that your CIO applies).

Hypercapitalism and the extended enterprise

The new competitive space is still capitalism. But its metabolism has been accelerated to become hypercapitalism. In the late 1990s Don Tapscott and others described this as a paradigm shift in which the unit of business extends out beyond the firm to become the extended enterprise. Borders were becoming porous, said Don. It's gone further now, he told us recently. Many borders are down.[4]

A business web is an elaborate network of suppliers, distributors, commercial services providers and customers that communicate and conduct transactions on the internet (or, increasingly, the emerging 'hypernet' of pervasive computing) in order to produce value for each other. It is a generic form of business relationship that is replacing the integrated corporation of the industrial economy. As a leader, you need to be aware which kind of web fits your business model. There are five, apparently.[5]

Spin your own web

The emergence of these new webs as proxies for the traditional corporation raises the question: Where are the boundaries that used to define a company? The 21st century company is defined by what happens at these edges, rather than 20th century notions of the corporate centre. The heart of an enterprise used to be at corporate HQ. Now, inspired organizations wear their heart on their sleeve. In creating a business web, the leader's job is to focus on what you do best and partner to do the rest; the old 'make or buy' issue. So, boundary issues become the central concerns of your business strategy. The dotcoms were a sideshow compared with the real next economy. The deep change wasn't about websites. It was and is about business webs and the relationships and alliances you form, both within and outside your organization.

Clearly, web-spinning is now part of your architectural toolkit. Your web needs to deliver flexibility, of course. But John Yard, until recently CIO at the UK's Inland Revenue, warns, 'People don't understand flexibility. It doesn't mean being able to jump any which way without boundary. It means creating an envelope of possibilities by thinking about trends (not specifics) and how they will impact your business, and then being flexible within that envelope. In other words, focus your flexibility or you end up all over the place.'

Flexible systems are M&A ready

Jan-Erik Gustavsson, a dream-team CIO who operates out of Scandinavia and London, adds some architectural tips here, too. If you are not the CIO, ask yours about M&A-ready systems; whether your systems are ready to deal with Mergers & Acquisitions and what you need to do to make them so. 'We can today build systems that are prepared for Mergers & Acquisitions, but no one does', says Jan-Erik. 'I don't understand why not. When an organization joins with another, systems are usually incompatible, but that doesn't have to be the case.'

We are heading towards the *terabit*[6] society where we can actually handle terabits per second. Between cities, this is still a physics problem, but it also represents challenges in networking and economics. And how the human mind will cope with that level and intensity of information is another question. 'We will need more sophisticated business models and management tools. We need to look at everything in real-time. We still need to develop different e-parameters and different management models to the old bricks and mortar world', advises Jan-Erik.

The number one challenge in architecting your IS system to allow you and your colleagues to lead flexibly and respond or anticipate in real-time is *complexity*. At the moment executives at all levels report that making a simple change at one end of a system can cause nightmares at the other. Small simple things can end up in the mire, as one small change impacts along the chain.

Think external customer control

Steve Parry, Head of Strategy at Fujitsu, adds one other principle: 'Think external customer control instead of internal hierarchical control. In other words, acknowledge when redesigning your system that the customer needs to be in control, which means (again) that decision making moves down to the front line, away from management. The front line is where the customers are. It's hard for many managers to acknowledge that their role is not to accumulate power anymore, but to support front line people in exercising their own decision making.'

Steve points to organizations such as Progressive Insurance in the US, which has re-invented how the claims side of motor insurance works by re-architecting its processes, its IS systems and the role of its people. At the heart of Progressive Insurance's process is proprietary software called Claims Workbench that allows fast, on-the-spot claims processing without resorting to a back office, breaking that industry's paradigm.

OK, that's enough about IS architecture: on to people ...

Increasingly, the question you have to ask yourself is, 'What's our human architecture?' Warren Bennis calls it your 'social architecture' and stresses that it has to be agile and adaptive.

Only the adaptable survive

'It is not the strongest of the species that survive, nor the most intelligent; it is the one that is most adaptable to change', said Darwin. Jesper Ejdling Martell, CEO & Co-Founder of Comintell, says that to make your organization more adaptable to change, and hence more likely to survive, you need to lead the development of intelligent workplace communities.

That's a group of people who share information, insight, experience and tools about an area of common interest. Virtual networks and teams of people often already exist in companies and form around topics of joint interest. The problem is, these groups are often very informal, non-documented, not adaptable to change and often based on personal networks – they converge around a personal need for information rather than the organization's need for information. How do you make this intelligent?

What is an intelligent community?

An intelligent community is a dynamic organism that quickly adapts to change in accordance with its surrounding environment and its past experiences. The key words are *quickly adapts to change*.

When Nokia announces a new phone, the technical people become interested. As time passes, other divisions like sales and marketing and then management become interested. As the product is launched, the community becomes very dynamic and everyone talks about it. But once it is launched, the internal community declines and shrinks as people lose interest.

The ability to shrink and expand is one definition of intelligent communities.

Structure

You have to put some sort of structure on a community to make it intelligent. Make it easy for people to join. Intelligent communities try to combine the best of the IT and HR departments, trying to bridge the gap between these two departments that traditionally never spoke to each other. 'Too much T in IT and too much R in HR was the problem at Ericsson, where I used to work, and it was about trying to get the two to speak to each other', says Jesper. Intranets are probably your key tool here.

The balancing act

Building an intelligent community is a balancing act. If it's too structured, you lose the creativity; if it's too creative then you lose the structure and the focus.

There are four balancing factors in developing an intelligent community

1   Is the knowledge explicit and can it be databased? Or is it implicit and in people's heads?

2   What is the degree of connection between the community members?

3   Should it be loose or should members be tightly controlled?

4   How closely can you integrate the community work with the everyday work? Ideally, knowledge management should be part of your everyday job – it shouldn't be an extra task.

The benefits

The benefits of intelligent communities are:

- improved decision making (see James Surowiecki's book *The Wisdom of Crowds* to destroy the myth of leader as 'best' decision maker: your intelligent communities will out-decision you every time);
- leveraged business competence;
- enhanced business productivity;
- trend-spotting and early warnings;
- re-use of knowledge;
- innovative environment;
- provision for rewards and career development; and
- strategic competence management.

The tacit mystery

Yes, we have sneaked you into knowledge management territory here, just when you thought you'd got through the book without being ambushed by KM or its variants too often. But, this isn't about KM as an IT discipline. Kjell Nordström, the Swedish economist, explains it by drawing a distinction between different kinds of knowledge.[7]

Articulate knowledge

Maths, engineering, sciences. It's recipe knowledge. This transferable knowledge is a limited competitive edge for you. The world is flooded with MBAs who have read the same books.

Tacit knowledge

This is where you know much more than you can say. 'My father's a fisherman in Finland. When we go out in his boat, he knows where the fish are', Dr Nordström told one of the authors in an interview recently. 'He knows it inside. He can't explain why. He just knows. A good sales person can do it but can't deliver a lecture on how they do it. According to the business schools and journals, if you can't say it or write it up, it doesn't exist. So, tacit knowledge isn't taught in schools.

'Old-fashioned managers value a McKinsey report full of facts and articulate knowledge more than tacit knowledge. They are wrong to do so. Tacit knowledge is now where competitive advantage comes from.'

What Mick Jagger knows that you don't

'The competitive advantage of an Ikea or a Southwest Airlines rests on a set of tacit principles. The Rolling Stones have built up a lot of tacit knowledge over 40 years. They just look at each other and they know to play "Satisfaction".

'Transferring tacit knowledge requires a lot of time with colleagues, picking up how they work. It's learning by mimicking, if you will. Think of it as mentorship over the course of years. Constantly reorganizing and splitting up teams stops tacit knowledge being passed on.'

Beware unwritten ground rules

We talked right at the beginning of this book about the importance of an organization being honest and true if you are not to develop too great a gap between the 'official' version of what the organization is and the actual culture. This is a vital part of creating a social architecture within which the 'Inspiration Virus' we referred to back in the opening chapter can thrive and spread.

It you're not clear what we mean by this distinction between official and unofficial culture, think of prisons and schools. Each has an official culture and an unofficial culture. Now remember your own school experience (we won't presume you have any prison experience to draw on) and how your context and the context of your fellow pupils was, in many cases, a subculture that was actually dominant in your day-to-day experience, compared with the official school structure and its accompanying rules of behaviour.

An Australian friend of ours, Steve Simpson, has created an acronym for this co-existence of an unofficial culture that exists below the leaders' radar or, in some cases, that leaders collude with while espousing the organization's official rules.

He calls the phenomenon UGRs, or Unwritten Ground Rules.

'UGRs are people's perceptions of the way we do things around here', Steve says. 'They are rarely explicit, but their power is enormous. UGRs are most prominent in casual discussions between staff, in the talk that occurs after meetings, and in the difference between what people say and what people do.'

UGRs may range from an implicit understanding that it's not worth raising new ideas that cost money, or that 'the boss' talks only to people who have done something wrong or interprets improvement suggestions from the front line as implied criticism and a challenge to his or her authority.

Research conducted at the University of Western Australia and Curtin University's Graduate School of Business confirms the power of the UGRs identified by Steve, and adds a layer of complexity by pointing out that different parts of the same workplace can have localized UGRs that deliver variants of the culture from department to department.

Common UGRs include:

1   At our meetings it isn't worth suggesting improvements because nothing will get done.
2   The only time anyone gets spoken to by the boss is when something is wrong.
3   The company talks about customer service, but we don't have to worry about it.
4   A lot of the jokes we tell each other are at the expense of colleagues, other departments or customers.
5   We go through the motions with our bosses, but once they have gone we do what we want, or have to do to get the job done.
6   New staff are not told about UGRs until they earn their stripes.[8]

We've talked in earlier chapters about ways of changing 'how the work works' to build in antibodies that prevent the emergence of the UGR tendency. Commitment-based management, Fernando Flores's approach that puts people at the heart of your organization and builds your business processes around the commitments they make to each other, is one. Systems thinking, where people have the power to redesign their own processes from the front line rather than having to cheat to meet top-down targets, is another.[9]

Changing 'the way the work works' is the central theme of this chapter – re-architecting what you do and how you do it, instilling leadership into all corners of your operation so people can act fast without constant reference back to the centre.

Founding principles

Hence the growing interest in founding principles as the cornerstone of your social architecture. Clearly articulated founding principles act as a constant guide to strategic and operational decision making, embedding leadership in the principles rather than in a person. Of course, a few organizations have both – leadership embedded in lived principles as well as embodied in an individual. Southwest Airlines and Herb Kelleher spring to mind, as do SWA's transatlantic equivalent, Virgin Atlantic and Richard Branson.

Here are the principles Richard Branson applies to leadership within Virgin Atlantic. How transferable are some of them to your organization's social architecture?

Richard's Guiding Principles

The foundation stones of Virgin Atlantic's social architecture

A copy of *Richard's Guiding Principles* is handed to every Virgin Atlantic employee:

- We must meet the passenger on his or her terms. They are individuals and require different things.
- As a rule we should be friendly and informal but always taking account of what the individual wants.
- Other airline staff are hidebound by rules. We should give ours guidelines and encourage them to solve a passenger's problem.

- First to know is best to deal with.
- The only way to make our staff trustworthy is to trust them. We must begin to trust people to use their judgement to resolve problems whilst being mindful of any costs to the Company.
- Mistakes are inevitable; dissatisfied customers are not.
- Our staff should be happy, cheerful, smiling, friendly and enjoying their job. It is a Manager's job to motivate the staff and create this atmosphere. Their role is to support their people in doing their best for the Passenger.
- Money is not the answer, good leadership is.
- We must give our staff responsibility and authority. Responsibility is the obligation to act, not just accept the blame. Authority is the resources to deal with the situation.
- We want our staff to bring their personalities to work and put them into their job. Bring individuality, freshness and care to their work.
- We need our staff to be comfortable with the exceptions, to think outside the framework and do what is right for the Passenger, not just 'the job'.
- We want our staff to anticipate a Passenger's problem. Think beyond the immediate, recognize the implications of their actions.
- The only purpose in having front line positions is if the passenger experiences service excellence. Otherwise why not use machines?
- We have two competitive advantages – product and service. We invest money and time in keeping our product different, fun, interesting and high quality. We must now invest in the same way for our service.
- We must communicate with our staff. If we change things we must tell them and tell them why.
- We must listen to what our staff have to say and act on it. If we can't do it we must say why not.
- We must improve in line with our culture, not at the expense of it.
- We must never design what we do by assuming the worst in people.

Source: Richard Branson's guiding principles for Virgin Atlantic staff.[10]

The upside-down organization

From Tom Peters to Leonard Berry to Ken Blanchard and other luminaries, there has been a lot of talk in leadership circles over the past decade of the need to turn your pyramid upside down; to see leadership as the support mechanism for the front line. It's the ultimate in re-architecting: picking the whole thing up and turning it on its head. Here's an example of how to do it from the UK:

Upside-down leadership
How to turn your organization on its head

Timpson is consistently in the top five of the annual *Sunday Times* '100 Best Companies to Work For' survey. At first glance, it is an unremarkable business – over 350 high street or mall-based stores offering key-cutting, engraving, watch and shoe repair services. Timpson celebrated its centenary in 2003. It looks like the kind of business where engrained old-fashioned practices would have been wiped out by a younger market entrant with fresher ideas.

In fact, Timpson is a thriving business because CEO John Timpson re-invented it from the inside before a newcomer could get there first.

The Timpson approach is based on 'upside-down management', which means giving responsibility and support to staff to make their own decisions. For example, store managers have freedom to:
- set prices – there is a price list, but it is just advisory;
- spend up to £500 resolving a complaint without escalating it – based on the idea that the cheapest settlements are always at source; and
- control and order stock.

Staff also have the freedom to test new ideas and ways of working. John puts it simply: 'If it works, tell us. If it doesn't, we suggest you stop doing it.'

This devolution of responsibility is reinforced through trust and training. All new store managers at Timpson are sent on a two-day residential induction course to learn 'how to be free'. From then on, individuals are in charge of their own training. The higher the skill levels they attain, the greater the bonuses they are entitled to.

No 'them' and 'us'. Just 'us'.

The company has architected its compensation package to resolve the conflict between the company's aim of keeping costs down and staff's natural desire to earn more. In most organizations this is a seed of conflict or, at best, creates two contexts instead of one. Timpson sets each store's turnover target at 4.5 times the wage bill. A staff bonus is then paid based on a proportion of any turnover above target. There's no upper limit and bonuses are paid weekly, which keeps people motivated.

John says of the bonus scheme: 'Our aim becomes helping our people earn more money. We've failed if they don't increase their take home pay substantially each year.' Compare that with organizations that look to keep the wage bill as low as possible.

Other staff benefits include a company pension scheme, financial hardship fund and the use of company holiday homes. This last idea was borrowed from Julian Richer of Richer Sounds, and it's used as a way of rewarding employees for five or more years' service.

The net result of this whole approach to management is that well over 90% of Timpson people report that 'our management trusts people to do a good job without looking over our shoulder' and that 'I can be myself around here'.

The difficult layer

... is often identified as the middle; in Timpson's case these are the area managers. Upside-down management says you delegate authority and keep responsibility. Too many middle managers do the reverse. So, Timpson is producing a small book to guide them. It's main message is, 'Your prime job is to praise people when they get it right. You should praise 10 times as much as you criticize.'

Source: John Timpson, CEO, Timpson Ltd.

The Ritz-Carlton hotel chain, with its principle of: 'We are ladies and gentlemen serving ladies and gentlemen', is another example of successfully inverting the pyramid. Founder and President Horst Schulze used to carry out the induction training at new hotels himself. He'd say to bellhops, room service waiters and chamber maids:

> 'I'm the President of this company, but you are far more important than me. If I don't turn up for work on a Monday morning, nobody cares. If you don't turn up for work, bags don't get carried, meals don't get served, beds don't get made. The place falls apart. So, who runs this place? Not me: you.'

And he meant it. Schulze gave everyone, including the bellhops, the power to spend up to $2,000 to please a customer, without reference to a manager. In practice, this didn't bankrupt the company; it helped turn it into an organization with a $1.2 billion operating budget that became the benchmark for service excellence in the hospitality industry.

At Bain & Co., the front line employees vote for who will be the top leader. At Prêt-à-Manger, sandwich-making employees successfully vetoed the appointment of a board-level director who spent the day in their store and failed to live the company values. In what ways have *you* turned the pyramid upside down?

Leaders and measurement

Traditional business valuation measures tell only part of the story. The value placed on new capabilities such as business agility and the emergence of new business forms such as the asset-less company have disrupted the old ways of valuing. Corporate analysts now factor in other intangibles such as Competitive Advantage Period (CAP), to try and deal with accelerated product cycles that leave shorter profit windows in which the cost of R&D can be recouped and profits made.[11]

The 21st century business leader has to manage an emerging set of metrics that investors are using to describe and assess options for growth – a forward indicator that is more useful

in times of great change than the traditional lagging indicators of past profit and loss. Whatever made you successful in
the past won't necessarily in the future, so replacing rear view
mirror business measures with forward-looking dashboards is
a competency that inspired leaders need the vision to oversee.
Commonly-agreed calculations for the value of a customer asset
base and its apparent loyalty are still slippery and need to become
more robust before they will break into the internationally-
agreed accounting conventions that still govern attempts to value
companies.[12]

As for measuring your corporation's ability to attract and retain
talent – putting a 'price' on your organization's talent leadership
capability – this is an even more amorphous area. Analysts factor
in top team talent and track record when valuing a company. But
it is not common to factor in the talent in an organization's overall
employee base as a factor of equivalent weight. In the absence of
established conventions, the best leaders appear to know instinctively how to manage these assets – an art traditionally not taught
or given little weight at business schools and one best codified and
learnt, therefore, through mediated peer learning; sharing new
leadership methods as they are forged, which our Network is helping to pioneer.

Soft is the new hard

Leadership in this new environment is about attracting and aligning groups of talented people to join forces to deliver previously-
thought-impossible results – whether these people are employed
by you or not is increasingly an irrelevance – and attracting the
best suppliers and a nexus of people who want to be your customers because they like the way you do business, or find the experience you offer irresistible. Regardless of whether Naomi Klein's
No Logo argument stands the test of time, 'Trust' has become the
new brand. Your people deliver it, not your advertising or your
logo designers.

Managing these intangible relationships is increasingly how
you deliver value. Interestingly, relationship management is traditionally seen as a feminine trait, yet only one of the FTSE 100

companies, at time of writing, is headed by a woman (Pearson's Marjorie Scardino).

If culture is the stuff of your social architecture – the way we do things around here – and the right culture can free people to excel, how do you measure it? Here's an example of how to move into the relatively unclaimed territory of measuring the soft stuff, from the Virgin empire's consumer finance arm, Virgin Direct:

How to measure behaviour

Virgin Direct has created a Performance Chart that is filled in weekly by members of the leadership team in a peer review.

It covers 20 or so behaviours that they all bought into as being essential for unleashing their people to excel. The three top managers rate each other out of five for each of the 20 behaviours, track variances, and decide on corrective action.

Scores have risen from an average of 3.1 to 4.2.

'It is a tool for making tangible behaviours that would otherwise not be measured. They become almost as "touchable" as sales figures', explains Inspired Leader Andrew Willey, Sales Director at Virgin Direct and Virgin Money.

Here are the principles that each person is scored against each week. How 'unleashed' do you think your people would be under a regime featuring this kind of leadership peer assessment and these principles?

The expected behaviours
Visionary
Loyal
Honest
Supporting
Open
Proactive
Listen and understand first before responding
Challenging
Positive and constructive
Coaching
Seen as 'one' (rather than conflicted or inconsistent)
Disciplined

Regular communication
Respect
Trusting
Professional
Robust thought and planned delivery
Fun

Each behaviour is scored weekly by peers:
0 No evidence
1 Sporadic evidence
2 Limited evidence
3 Minimum standard
4 Good
5 Flawless

Source: Andrew Willey, Sales Director, Virgin Direct and Virgin Money

Size matters: small is the new big

Maybe E F Schumacher was right: small is beautiful. When we look at how our Network members build agility, responsiveness and entrepreneurship into a big, lumbering organization, an increasing number do so by breaking their giant, unwieldy tanker into a flotilla of small ships. Here's an example from Larissa Joy, COO at Weber Shandwick:

Nine dwarfs are more agile than one giant

'We divided into nine units, each led by an entrepreneurial leader, with responsibility for revenue, people and clients', said Larissa when we asked her to explain her approach to building in agility. Larissa's actions here fit the current Branson-inspired wisdom for building agility and *esprit de corps*; that 200 or so is the optimum number of employees per business unit.

Create hit squads to clear sclerotic arteries

'We set up a series of temporary teams that meet to create breakthroughs in individual areas that need tackling, from employee issues to cost-saving measures. We call them "star" teams. They pull together high-performing people, with a tightly-defined, clear role and a leader. For example, one star team shaved £1.5 million from our overheads in a short period of time, with no noticeable client impact, then disbanded.'

There's been a lot of talk of the need to become a 'fast company', particularly throughout the late 1990s. But Larissa warns that if you apply this principle to your decision making, you can end up grinding to a halt. Agile organizations aren't always making snap decisions.

The quick and the dead

'There's a confusion between short-term results and short-term decisions', says Larissa. 'When there is enormous pressure to make your quarterly shareholder results, there's a tendency among leaders to take decisions quickly, on their own. They think that's what leadership is: making the tough decisions alone. Er, WRONG. Making fast decisions behind closed doors just alienates the people who have to carry out those decisions. It's better to get the buy-in rather than take the short cut. It takes longer, but you get better quality, more actionable decisions.'

We talked, above, about M&A-ready IS systems. Larissa has a great anecdote about how not to become a leader of one of the 75% of M&As that fail to deliver any value.[13] Because, ultimately, it's the people who deliver the value in Mergers & Acquisitions, unless the merger is about consolidating a crowded supply side to reduce customer choice. 'We merged two companies, but let them continue in separate premises', said Larissa. 'Big mistake. I'll never do that again. We tried, and failed, to get them to interact; to talk and work together. They just stayed in their respective buildings. The next step would have been outward-bound team-building courses, all that sort of stuff.

'But we tried something different. We built a bar in the reception area of one of the buildings. And we took all the money we would have spent on external courses and put it behind the bar. It was very simple. They all sat down together, got to know each other over free drinks and the merger became much more successful.

People work well together because they trust each other. They trust each other because they know each other. This was a way of bringing them together to start that process. It's easy to forget how scared people can be of a merger.'

And, finally ...

Just how important is inspired leadership and the architecting that allows it to spread? We have to bow to the wisdom of our associate member Warren Bennis here, since he's written 27 books on leadership and virtually invented it as an academic discipline. Warren tells us this: 'All the studies I have looked at find that leadership is responsible for roughly 15% of a corporation's success. The thing is that in highly competitive times like the ones we are experiencing now, that 15% can be the make or break factor.

'Leaders don't emerge like Venus out of the sea. If you want to create leadership at every level, leaders at the top have to create the systems and culture that allow that to happen. Authoritarian leaders want predictability; to control the uncontrollable ... 21st century leaders realize they are part of an overall agenda, not the master of it.'

If you take away just two things from this book, these are the two things we recommend you take away: The first bit's about you; Be true to yourself and your values. Pretending you're someone you're not will make life at work far more complicated than it should be, and you will be much less effective as a leader. The second bit is about the people you lead: connect results with people so they can see how their actions contribute directly to the organization.

Oh, and a third, of course. Come and join us if you think you're inspired enough (or potentially inspired enough): http://www.inspiredleaders.com. We look forward to hearing from you ...

This chapter drew on the practice and thinking of the following members and friends of the Inspired Leaders Network
Professor Paul Strassmann
IT economist; former CIO, the US Defense Department and Xerox Corporation.

Don Tapscott
Digital guru.

Jennifer Mowatt
Former Country Manager, eBay UK.

John Timpson
CEO, Timpson Ltd.

Cedric Read
Cedric was head of Pricewaterhouse's Financial Management practice and has been one of the most respected voices on what Finance Directors or Chief Financial Officers should be doing for years. He is co-author of the books *CFO Insight, The CFO as Business Integrator* and *eCFO*.

Jan-Erik Gustavsson
Dreamteam CIO at Boo.com and letsbuyit.com (he never bought any stock in the companies and their technology was widely-admired). Jan-Erik is now a technology entrepreneur. One of his companies, Telefortress AB, offers IS survival backup services based under the mountains in a remote area of Sweden. Very James Bond.

Sir Nick Scheele
President and COO, Ford Motor Company.

John Yard
Until recently CIO at the UK's Inland Revenue Department.

Steve Parry
Head of Strategy, Fujitsu.

Warren Bennis
The Dean of Leadership.

Jim Sterne
Founder and Principal, Target Marketing, Santa Barbara, author of *Customer Service On The Internet*.

Larissa Joy
COO, UK & Continental Europe, Weber Shandwick.

Jesper-Ejdling Martell
CEO and co-founder, Comintell Inc. Jesper created the Corporate Business Information Centre at Ericsson, regarded by those in the know as one of the most effective competitive intelligence systems in the world.

Andrew Willey
Sales Director, Virgin Direct and Virgin Money.

Afterword: Who Inspires Us?

When we ask the Inspired Leaders Network members 'Who inspires you?', here are some of the better-known names that recur most often. We are delighted to be able to say that some are members or friends of our network: 'On giants' shoulders', as Newton said …

Tom Peters*, Warren Bennis, Anita Roddick (*The Body Shop*), Stephen Covey, Herb Kelleher (*Southwest Airlines*), Meg Whitman (*eBay*), Richard Branson (*Virgin*), Martin Luther King, Dee Hock (*Visa*), Winston Churchill, Ricardo Semler (*Semco SA*), Gandhi, Rupert Murdoch (*News International*), E F Schumacher, Steve Jobs (*Apple*), Fernando Flores, Jan Carlzon (*Scandinavian Airline Systems*), Edward De Bono, Walt Disney, Charles Dunstone (*Carphone Warehouse*), Andy Taylor (*Enterprise Rent-A-Car*), Terry Leahy (*Tesco*), Nelson Mandela, Sam Walton (*Wal-Mart*), Jack Welch (*General Electric*), Andy Grove (*Intel*), Kjell Nordström & Jonas Ridderstråle, Charles Handy, Fred Smith (*Federal Express*), John F Kennedy, Tim Brown (*IDEO*), Jeff Bezos (*Amazon*), Lou Gerstner *(IBM*), Michael Porter, Val Gooding (*BUPA*), Bill Gates (*Microsoft*), Fred Reichheld, Guy Kawasaki (*Garage*), Nick Scheele (*Ford*), Simon Woodroffe (*YO! Sushi*), Michael Dell (*Dell*), Robert K Cooper, James Dyson (*Dyson*), Ingvar Kamprad (*IKEA*), Gary Hamel, Colleen Barrett (*Southwest Airlines*), Feargal Quinn (*Superquinn)*, Captain Mike Abrashoff (*US Navy*), Horst Schulze (*Ritz-Carlton Hotels*), Tim Sanders (*Yahoo!*), Peter Lewis (*Progressive Insurance*), Martin Sorrell (*WPP*), Howard Schultz (*Starbucks*), Don Peppers (*Peppers & Rogers*), Sinclair Beecham & Julian Metcalfe (*Pret A Manger*).

*Thank you in particular to Tom Peters. After attending a seminar that Tom gave in the late 1990s, the founders of the Inspired

Leaders Network, Meenu Bachan and Phil Blackburn, thought 'Wouldn't it be incredible to get together a network of the kinds of leaders Tom talks about – leading edge people who are pioneering how business will be done rather than copying others – and get them to share what they are doing and how they are doing it.' And that's how The Inspired Leaders Network started.

So come join us

Help us spread the inspiration virus. Visit the Inspired Leaders Network at www.inspiredleaders.com to pick up more bite-sized inspiration from some of the leaders featured in this book – and others we couldn't fit into its pages. The site contains details of how you can join us, which entitles you to attend our Inspired Leaders Network sessions and/or take part virtually in sharing the techniques and practices of your fellow members …

Notes

Preface

1 Jim Collins, *Good to Great.*

2 Dr Stephen Covey, *The Seven Habits of Highly Effective People and The 8th Habit: From Effectiveness to Greatness.*

Secret 1

1 A publication from the UK Government's Department of Trade and Industry, which drew on our research. The statistics mentioned in the *Guardian* report are based on a survey of over 1,500 managers carried out by the Chartered Management Institute.

2 The Gallup Organization's annual research into employee engagement.

3 Crawford Hollingworth, CEO, Headlight Vision.

4 *New Scientist* magazine, September 2004.

5 UK Chartered Management Institute survey of over 1,500 managers, 2004.

6 Taylor had a breakdown from overwork and died the day after his 59th birthday in 1915. The father of time and motion studies died as he was winding his watch. See Anita Roddick and David Boyle's book *Numbers.*

7 Source: Don Tapscott, a member of our Network, citing research for his book *Growing Up Digital.*

8 *Managers and Leaders: Are They Different?* by Abraham Zaleznik, 1977 (*HBR* reprint 92211).

9   Actually, 'post-modern' as a concept is itself getting a bit tired, isn't it? Maybe we mean post-post-modern. But, seriously … inspired leaders are not bound by the misleading concept of linear progression; of modern management or leadership methods being automatically more informed and inspired than traditional truths. They look forward, backwards and sideways for their own inspiration.

10   Source: Network member Richard Whiteley, founder of The Forum Corporation and co-author of *Customer Centered Growth.*

11   Tom Peters, talking at the North American Conference on Customer Management, Orlando, Fla, November, 2003.

12   These categories are from the UK Government's publication *Inspired Leadership, an Insight Into People Who Inspire Exceptional Performance,* October, 2004, towards which we contributed.

Secret 2

1   Neil Croft's book *Authentic: How To Make A Living By Being Yourself,* (Capstone, 2003) is just one of the texts on authenticity, integrity and living a true life as people search for deeper meaning.

2   More on Bill Hicks's unique, albeit now posthumous, contribution to the authenticity debate here: www.billhicks.com.

3   Gallup Organization's Marcus Buckingham *et al., First Break All The Rules* (Simon & Schuster, 2000) and *Now Discover Your Strengths* (Free Press, 2002).

4   Research carried out by John Tschohl, The Service Quality Institute, Minneapolis. www.customer-service.com

5   Don is the co-author, with business partner Martha Rogers, of all those *One to One* books. He is founding partner at Peppers & Rogers. The editor of *Inc.* magazine called their first book, *The One to One Future,* 'one of the two or three most important business books of all time'. www.1to1.com

6   Basically put, well looked-after staff leads to well looked-after customers, and that leads to a quantifiable increase in profit. See the Harvard Business Press paper *Putting The Service Profit Chain To Work* by Heskett, Sasser *et al.,* July 1, 2000.

7   Quoted in *Fast Company Magazine,* October 1996.

8   Don Peppers was addressing the Inspired Leaders Network's annual summer dinner at the Tanaka Business School, London.

9   David Grayson is author of *Corporate Social Opportunity*, Greenleaf Publishing, July 2004.

Secret 3

1   Inflation adjusted per-capita American income has more than doubled since 1960, meaning that the typical person now commands twice the buying power their father or mother had in the year 1960. During the 1950s, a cheeseburger at McDonald's cost the typical person half an hour of wages; now the typical American can buy a McDonald's cheeseburger for the price of three minutes of wages. For more see *The Progress Paradox: How Life Gets Better While People Feel Worse,* Gregg Easterbrook, Random House, 2003.

2   Nordström & Ridderstråle argue powerfully for the need to harness the power of attraction and for its growing role as a success factor at all levels, from individuals to organizations to national regions, to nations to groups of nations such as the European Economic Union. Those who can attract the best people, customers, reputation, investors, resources, win. See *Funky Business.*

3   The average value of a UK home doubled between the beginning of 2000 and the start of 2004. UK home owners have been investing their new capital in second or retirement homes in Europe in such numbers that they have distorted domestic house price movements in those countries; in effect exporting the UK's house price inflation. In Languedoc Roussillon, for example, the average house price increase in 2003 was around 28%, almost triple the French national average. Research by Barclays puts this down to demand for French homes by Britons. Similarly, 40% of all new homes sold on the Spanish costas in 2003 were bought by Britons.

4   Henry actively puts into practice the principles of South American entrepreneur Ricardo Semler, who virtually handed over the running of his company, SEMCO, to his people. Semler once returned from a year's sabbatical and found his office and

desk had been handed over to someone else in his absence. 'I'm still trying to get it back', we heard Semler say recently at a conference in London. See his books *Maverick* and *The Seven Day Weekend*.

5   Rolf Jensen, the Danish futurist and author of *The Dream Society*, says that the future belongs to the companies with the best stories. He doesn't mean PR. He means the company as a story, a continuous narrative that gives meaning to the people who work there and who buy from it or invest in it. The NHS has its own story. Virgin has its own story. Virgin's story happens to have a beard.

6   Quoted by Tom Peters, speaking at the European Conference on Customer Management in London, May, 2003.

7   For a primer on the language of 21st century inspired business leadership, see the *Cluetrain Manifesto* on www.cluetrain.com. Here's the essence: 'A powerful global conversation has begun. Through the internet, people are discovering and inventing new ways to share relevant knowledge with blinding speed. As a direct result, markets are getting smarter – and getting smarter faster than most companies. These markets are conversations. Their members communicate in language that is natural, open, honest, direct, funny and often shocking. Whether explaining or complaining, joking or serious, the human voice is unmistakably genuine. It can't be faked. Most corporations, on the other hand, only know how to talk in the soothing, humourless monotone of the mission statement, marketing brochure, and your-call-is-important-to-us busy signal. Same old tone, same old lies. No wonder networked markets have no respect for companies unable or unwilling to speak as they do.'

8   Jon Johnson, Professor of Management, Sam M. Walton College of Business, University of Arkansas. Quoted by Richard Reeves at one of our events.

9   *It's Your Ship! Management Techniques From The Best Damn Ship In The Navy*, by Captain D Mike Abrashoff, formerly commander of the *USS Benfold*. Abrashoff charts his techniques for shifting the culture 'from obedience to performance'. 'The most important thing a captain can do is see the ship through the eyes of the crew', he says.

10   See *The War For Talent*, Ed Michaels *et al.*, Harvard Business School, for more on EVPs.

Secret 4

1   In his book of the same name, *The Innovator's Dilemma, 1997*, recently followed by the satisfyingly titled *The Innovator's Solution*.

2   Mike Harris, founding CEO of the pioneering bank First Direct, subsequently co-founder of the digital bank Egg, says the trick is to be able to spot when a business form or customer proposition is about to run out of steam, then abandon it in favour of the revolutionary new one you've been quietly building in the back. Mike recommends using a number of tools such as System Dynamics, developed at MIT, to help you gauge when to jump. As ever, timing is all. More from Mike on this in the chapter titled 'The Impossible Isn't'.

3   OK, at various points in this book the sharp reader will note that we describe inertia, denial, the need to be in control, love, hate and one or two other things as each 'the most powerful force in the universe'. How can they all be, you ask? Each statement is only invalidated by the other if you think we mean *at the same time*. They take it in turns.

4   Authored by Dave Allan, Matt Kingdon, Kristina Murrin *et al.* If you buy this, don't also buy *?WhatIf! How to start a creative revolution at work*. Although it's almost as good, it's bound to be, since it's an older version of the same book.

5   We'd also recommend:

   • *Smart Things To Know About Innovation*, Dennis Sherwood, Capstone. Sherwood is the originator of the phrase 'premature evaluation', which we use in this chapter – the common practice of throwing ideas out too early or betting the farm on an idea that turns out subsequently not to work.

   • *Aha!* Jordan Ayan and Rick Benzel, Crown Publications. See, that one's not a Capstone publication

6   If you want to know more about improv and business creativity, try the *Applied Improvisation Network* www.appliedimprov. net and Johnnie Moore on www.johnniemoore.com.

7   Before you get picky about our scientific knowledge and allow that scepticism to undermine your faith in the other assertions and arguments we make in this book, you should know that between 50% and 99% of an iceberg is under water, the level of buoyancy being determined by the balance between the amount of air trapped in it versus frozen dead mammoths and other ballast.

8   Hamish was recently (he's just left to set up a new airline) CEO of Vision Consulting, which helps organizations put into practice the fascinating ideas of Chilean Senator Fernando Flores. More on those ideas in the chapter headed 'The Impossible Isn't'. Hamish was CEO of Eurostar Group, where he drew on his time as brand manager at British Airways to model the Eurostar train service on a plane service. He was also the CEO of Sainsbury's Bank, pioneering the selling of car loans and credit cards within supermarkets. Here's another example from Hamish of looking outside your own industry for established but hidden leading edge practice: 'I spent some time with head teachers, learning how they win over rebellious or disruptive pupils, and came away with some powerful ideas for how to re-enlist employees who had grown disillusioned with an organization and were no longer aligned with it.'

9   See note 5 for details of Sherwood's book, which is one of our recommended reads on innovation.

10   You'll find more words of wisdom from Simon in his great little book *The Book of Yo!* OK, yes it is published by Capstone, but that's still just a coincidence.

Secret 5

1   The late Cyril Gates, former Customer Services Director at BBC Resources used to say, 'This is an age in which you have to create for customers an experience they can touch, see, hear, taste, feel and even step in.'

2   Harley-Davidson executives love repeating this quote. It first appeared, to our knowledge, in the book *Results-Based Leadership*, by Ulrich, Zenger and Smallwood. John is the third HD senior executive we've heard use it, Richard Teerlink and

John's predecessor Clyde Fessler being the other two. But, it's such a brilliant quote, it bears repeating.

3   *The Experience Economy*, Joseph Pine, James Gilmore *et al.*, 1999.

4   What De Bono actually said, to The American Society of Editors' Conference in 1997, was: 'For the last nine years Ford Motor Company has made more money not by selling cars, but by lending people money to buy cars. Ford is a bank that only makes cars to get customers.' You only have to look at the power of GE Capital to realize that selling money is more profitable than selling things.

5   Recent research suggests the explosion of consumer hyper-choice leads to anxiety and decision paralysis. In his book *The Paradox of Choice: Why More Is Less* (HarperCollins, July 2004), Barry Schwartz cites the 285 varieties of cookies (21 of them chocolate chip), 61 varieties of suntan oil or sunblock and 230 kinds of soup facing him every time he visits his supermarket.

6   Krispy Kreme, which you can now buy in Harrods in London, incidentally. 'We view the experience of a Krispy Kreme store as the defining element of the brand', Scott Livengood, CEO, told Shaun Smith, author of *Branding The Customer Experience*.

7   Sources for these examples: Lyell Strambi, COO, Virgin Atlantic and www.virgin.com

8   Source: Publicly available Harley-Davidson trading figures.

9   W Edwards Deming, the American statistician who originated methods such as statistical process control. Deming's ideas at first received more attention in Japan than in his home country. He was invited to tour Japan and lectured extensively there, providing much of the thinking that drove the quality revolution achieved by Japanese manufacturers. Japan's highest quality award is named after him. It was only after the success Japanese manufacturers had with his methods that the West began paying more attention to what Deming had been saying.

10   John Seddon is the sharpest thinker we know on the whole subject of systems thinking and how to redesign the way your work works. He has inspired a number of our members. See

his book *Freedom From Command And Control: A better way to make the work work*. www.lean-service.com

11   Wendy Thomson, Head of the UK Prime Minister's Office of Public Services Reform and one of our members, points out that imposing targets from the top is only the first phase of public services reform, which gives way to bottom-up reform once customers are integrated into the system.

12   Between 70% and 80% of Mergers & Acquisitions fail to deliver shareholder value, according to KPMG ('Worldclass Transactions: Insights into creating shareholder value through mergers and acquisitions', 2001).

13   Carlzon's book was first published in 1989. He called these encounters with a brand 'Moments of Truth', as it is these experiences that dictate how a customer feels about the brand. When General Motors set up the carmaker Saturn it identified 150 Moments of Truth and tried to create action plans to manage them. The company later scaled this back to a more manageable 40, including items such as:

   1   Exposure to a TV ad

   18   Customer wants to bring car in for service. Is the dealer open?

   32   Customer experiences first parking lot dent.

   The *Daily Telegraph* newspaper, which felt Saturn went over the top in trying to cover every eventuality, claimed to have found four missing moments, including:

   41   Customer meets aliens from a different galaxy.

   42   Customer metamorphoses into a marsupial and regards this as a negative event.

   43   Customer drives a European car and notices the difference.

   (*Daily Telegraph*, March 20, 1999)

14   Q: What is the fourth largest company in Thailand and also the number one retailer in Hungary?

   A: Tesco. *Management Today*, February 2004.

15   Sir Terry Leahy is Britain's Most Admired Business Leader, according to a survey by the UK magazine *Management Today*. There's something of a debate on at the moment about what type of person makes a great leader. Leahy fits the 'Quiet

Leader' type promoted by Jim Collins in his book *Good to Great* as being the kind of leader whose lack of apparent ego plus a willingness to put the company and its stakeholders first brings long-term success. Journalist Chris Blackhurst writes of Leahy in *MT*, February 2004: 'In a society that likes its tycoons to be overbearing figures, he's so, well, ordinary. His shirt isn't loud. He refuses to allow status and wealth to go to his head. He drives his own car to work, doesn't keep a large support staff, won't take outside directorships, replies to questions about the cult of personality with, "The only personality I believe in is Tesco". Blink and you would miss him. He's a blur in the background on school photos.'

16   Richard Duvall, formerly Chief Marketing Officer, Egg. For more on the erosion of the Richness vs Reach trade-off, read *Blown To Bits*, by Philip Evans & Thomas Wurster, Harvard Business School Press 1999.

17   *Real Time: Preparing For The Age of The Never-Satisfied Customer.* Regis McKenna, Harvard Business School Press 1997.

18   Fred Reichheld told one of the authors in an interview, 'I've given up on customer satisfaction surveys.' It was Reichheld's book, *The Loyalty Effect*, that started businesses thinking about customer retention as a route to growth in a big way back in 1996. It is now well known that, as Reichheld made clear then, satisfied customers defect, too. One of our Network members, Carphone CEO Charles Dunstone, echoes Reichheld's finding that there is just one question you should be asking your customers that is more significant than any other. Instead of a satisfaction survey, poll them with this one question: 'Would you recommend us to a friend?'

19   Dow is fond of telling this story at conferences. Thanks to Don Peppers for sharing it. See Dow's book *Turned On: Eight Vital Insights To Energize Your People, Customers And Profits*, Harper-Collins 1996.

Secret 6

1   Peter Drucker, writing in *The Economist*, noted this about the future of multinationals: 'Multinationals now tend to be organized globally along product or service lines. But like the multi-

nationals of 1913, they are held together and controlled by ownership. By contrast, the multinationals of 2025 are likely to be held together and controlled by strategy. There will still be ownership, of course. But alliances, joint ventures, minority stakes, know-how agreements and contracts will increasingly be the building blocks of a confederation. This kind of organization will need a new kind of top management.' 'The Near Future Survey', *The Economist*, 2 November, 2001.

2   Network member Andrew Fraser points out that a nationalist perspective of winners and losers can be deceptive, just as using nation-based language doesn't allow your mental model of global business enough flexibility. He and others posit 'Wimbledonisation' as an example of how you can win when you appear to be losing on the global stage. It doesn't matter if 'foreigners' win all the prizes. It's who stages the tournament that wins.

3   Einstein was righter than he knew. Everything is relative. Perspective gives you a partial picture. Commentators in the UK and US focus on the loss of white collar jobs to emerging countries – insurance back-office jobs shifting to Delhi, programmers in Bangalore writing for clients on the West Coast of the US. Yet, if you are the minister for health in the Philippines, the challenge of globalism, for you, is that developed countries appear to be poaching your precious professional classes, with the nurses and doctors you paid to train up leaving to support the hospital system in the UK and elsewhere.

4   Nordström and his fellow economist Jonas Ridderstråle expand on this argument in their books *Funky Business* and *Karaoke Capitalism*. Network member David Grayson echoes some of the Swedish economists' popularizing of the notion of 'tribes' being increasingly important as market segments compared with traditional segmentation by geography. 'Demographics are no longer a sensible way of segmenting your customers. And geography is no longer a sufficient way of carving up your global business responsibilities ("You take Africa, I'll take North America")', says David. 'It is increasingly easy for us to identify with like-minded people, even if they are on a different continent. And the consequences for

business are that one needs to think not merely about our relationship with physical communities, but our relationships with communities of interest – environmental campaigners, for example – and communities of identity, for example African-American employees and so on.'

5   Source of these statistics: Andrew Fraser, Mitsubishi and Anita Roddick, founder, The Body Shop. See Anita and David Boyle's book *Numbers*, available through www.anitaroddick. com, for more eye-opening numbers; some sobering, others enlightening.

6   From a paper written and presented to an invitation-only audience of Andersen Consulting (now Accenture) employees, partners and their clients, by Bob Geldof, West London, 2001.

Secret 7

1   The Schopenhauer and Abraham Herschel quotes in this chapter are both quoted in Robert K. Cooper's brilliant book *The Other 90%. How to unlock your vast untapped potential for leadership and life,* Crown Business, 2001.

2   The science of complexity offers great hope for leadership in all dimensions in the future. One book that is a great introduction to the subject is the readable *The Intelligence Advantage,* by Michael D McMaster, Butterworth-Heinemann 1996. More academic is *Open Boundaries,* by Howard J. Sherman & R. Schultz, Perseus Books Group 1999.

3   'Every quarter or so we model our own strategy (using MIT's system dynamics) to see where it will take us in three or four years. As a result, we've re-invented the business twice to move away from a strategy before it had exhausted itself. Cycles of re-invention in the private sector look to me to be every three years or so now', says Mike.

4   Tracy Goss is one of the foremost authorities on Organizational and Executive Re-Invention, having pioneered and shaped this field over twenty years. President of Goss Reid Associates, Inc., a management consulting firm based in Austin, Texas, she is the author of *The Last Word on Power: Executive Re-Inven-*

tion for Leaders Who Must Make the Impossible Happen which we always recommend to Inspired Leaders Network members as a must-read. http://www.re-invention.com/.

5   *Confronting Reality: Master The New Model For Success*, Larry Bossidy & Ram Charan, Random House, 2004.

6   www.debonogroup.com

7   We traced this story back to Joe Rohde, a senior creative executive at Disney, and an explorer who sports a handlebar mustache and an elongated ear lobe, stretched by a string of shells and bones collected from his visits to tribal villages in Africa, Thailand and Nepal. 'He once brought a tiger on a leash into a meeting with Disney CEO Michael Eisner, to illustrate the allure of live animals. Stunned, and no doubt impressed, Eisner gave Rohde the go-ahead for Animal Kingdom, Walt Disney World's fourth theme park', it says in the Disney online talk forum on these pages. It's fascinating reading: www.talkdisney.com/forums/archive/index.php/t-3585.html

8   Try *Crossing The Unknown Sea: Work And The Shaping of Identity*, Penguin, 2004, or *The Heart Aroused: Poetry and the Preservation of The Soul in Corporate America* (or … *of The Soul At Work*, depending on which side of the Atlantic you are on), Doubleday, 1996, both by David Whyte.

9   *Open Boundaries*, by Sherman & Schultz (see note 2) contains a brilliant chapter on how to sell radical change to a traditional workforce.

10 *Built to Last: Successful Habits of Visionary Companies*, James Collins & Jerry Poras, HarperCollins, 1994.

11 *Re-Imagine: Business Excellence In a Disruptive Age*, Tom Peters, Dorling-Kindersley, 2003.

12 *Fast Company*, January 1999. As an aside, ever wondered where Donald Rumsfeld got all that stuff he was struggling to say about the things we know and the things we think we know and the things we don't know we don't know …? From Flores, quite possibly. 'The World According to Flores exists in three realms', wrote Harriet Rubin in *Fast Company*. 'The first is the smallest – and the most self-limiting: What You Know You Know. It is a self-contained world, in which people are

unwilling to risk their identity in order to take on new challenges. A richer realm is What You Don't Know – the realm of uncertainty, which manifests itself as anxiety or boredom. Most things in life belong to this realm: what you don't know about your future, your health, your family. People are always trying to merge this second area into the realm of What You Know You Know – in order to avoid uncertainty, anxiety, and boredom. But it is the third realm of Flores' taxonomy to which people should aspire: What You Don't Know You Don't Know. To live in this realm is to notice opportunities that have the power to reinvent your company, opportunities that we're normally too blind to see. In this third realm, you see without bias: You're not weighed down with information. The language of this realm is the language of truth, which requires trust'.

13   Tom Peters speaking at the European *Conference on Customer Management* in London, May 2003.

14   Source: Charles Spinosa, co-author with Fernando Flores of *Disclosing New Worlds: Entrepreneurship, Democratic Action and the Culture of Solidarity*, MIT Press, 1997.

15   Black, DH & Synan, CD, *The Learning Organization, the Sixth Discipline*. Quoted in *The Innovation Wave, Addressing Future Challenges*, Bettina von Stamm, John Wiley & Sons, 2002.

Conclusion and Bonus Secret 8

1   Paul says there are 12 key determinants of competitive success. The 12 ingredients are enshrined in the PIMS programme (which stands for the Profit Impact of Market Strategies), started in 1965 by General Electric and now run by the Strategic Planning Institute out of Cambridge, Mass. 'The essence of leadership lies in how an individual leader balances and mixes the ingredients of strategic influence to deliver the most effective results', says Paul. For a quick thumbnail of these factors, we've listed below Paul's summary of the PIMS database's 12 key determinants of competitive success. The tabulation indicates which conditions are either favourable or unfavourable to profitability.

KEY DETERMINANTS OF COMPETITIVE SUCCESS

Favourable	Strategic Influence	Unfavourable
Differentiated	Product or service	Commodity
Segmented	Served market	Unsegmented
High	Relative market share	Low
High	Relative product quality	Low
Low	Relative costs	High
Good	Operating effectiveness	Poor
Low	Investment intensity	High
Substantial	Perceived quality	Thin
Growing	Value added	Shrinking
Positive	Growth rate	Flat or negative
High	SG&A and R&D	Low
New	Age of assets	Old

This table first appeared in *Leader to Leader* magazine, a publication of the Peter Drucker Foundation, in 2002. Notice any mention of people in the table? No, neither did we.

2   See *Pyramids Are Tombs: Traditional Corporate Structure, Like The 20th Century, is History*, by Joe Phelps, IMC 2002.

3   Nordström & Ridderstråle, *Funky Business*.

4   *Digital Capital: Harnessing The Power of Business Webs*, by Don Tapscott *et al.*, Harvard Business School Press.

5   The five types of Business Web identified by Don are:

- *Value Chains* and *Alliances* add value by converting raw materials or ideas into finished goods.
- *Aggregations* and *Agoras* select, package and price goods for markets they seek out.
- *Distributive Networks* service these other four by allocating and delivering goods from providers to users.

Source: Don Tapscott

6   In measuring data transmission speed, a *terabit* is one trillion binary digits, or 1,000,000,000,000 (that is, 10 to the power of 12) bits. A terabit is a measure of the amount of data that is transferred in a second between two points. As opposed to

terabyte, which is a measure of storage equal to a thousand gigabytes. It's how fast it moves that counts.

7   For more inspiration from the brilliant bald Swede and his glimmer twin* Jonas Ridderstråle, read two of our favourite books, which are referred to many times in these notes: *Funky Business* and *Karaoke Capitalism*. Reading them is a little like being plugged into the mains. (*Mick Jagger and Keith Richards used to be called 'The Glimmer Twins' and the two Swedes are the guru world's equivalent, in case that reference passed you by.)

8   For more on this see Steve's illuminating but hard-to-find book *Unwritten Ground Rules: Cracking the Corporate Culture Code*. If you can't find it on Amazon, try his website on www. keystone-management.com.

9   As mentioned earlier in the book, do a Google search on John Seddon to find out more about systems thinking and how to apply it in your organization: he's the sharpest practitioner and most eloquent champion of systems thinking as a way of doing business that we know. Public sector and not-for-profits: this is for you, too.

10 Our friend Chris Daffy first published these principles in his powerful book *Once A Customer Always A Customer*, Oak Tree Press. A colleague at Virgin tells us they no longer circulate 'Richard's Guiding Principles', but 'maybe we should, it's great'.

11 Cedric Read's research among leading global CFOs underpins this section on new metrics. He is the lead author of *eCFO: Sustaining Value In The New Corporation*, published by John Wiley & Sons Ltd.

12 Jim Sterne of Target Marketing in Santa Barbara (author of *Customer Service On The Internet*) is pioneering work in this area.

13 A reminder from Secret 5: Between 70% and 80% of Mergers & Acquisitions fail to deliver shareholder value, according to KPMG ('Worldclass Transactions: Insights into creating shareholder value through mergers and acquisitions', 2001).

Index